PRAYING L I K E JESUS

"Lord, teach us to pray."
LUKE 11:1B

www.walnuthillcc.org

Acknowledgements

There are so many who have contributed to the development of this prayer course. A project of this magnitude would not have been possible without the help of many, and I'm so grateful to all those who have left their mark on this body of work. It is a true community effort. A very heartfelt thank you to Lindsey the Bold, Karen the Brave, Lynne the Lionhearted, Vicky the Valiant, Barb the Benevolent, Cynthia the Serene, Anna Mae the Excellent, and Parker the Brilliant. Thank you all for your service to the King.

AJ PICARD
PASTOR OF PRAYER

TABLE OF CONTENTS

USING THE CURRICULUM

What an honor to come alongside you in what is truly a most noble quest — learning to pray like Jesus. The following pages will assist you in this journey.

First, this workbook provides you with weekly group sessions that will be led by your group leader. Each group session contains key learnings for the week that you'll uncover with your group leader, along with a link to each week's video short that you'll watch together. Additionally, you will have five daily devotional entries each week with corresponding journal exercises. The intention is not to give you more to do in your already busy life. This is not a religious duty but a place of encounter with God. The quest you are on in learning to pray is caught more than taught, so these daily journal exercises are intended to help you cultivate an authentic and vibrant prayer life.

You will do this by engaging in honest questions and creative prayer activities following each of the entries. You'll also practice praying together in group sessions. Your leader is here to encourage you in your quest by helping you practice what you're learning in prayer, both as a group and on your own with God. Group sessions are intended to be a place where you can unpack what you are learning on the journey, ask questions, and have the time and space to share with one another.

The wisdom of this prayer course is rooted in the Word of God, so you'll be digesting a healthy amount of Scripture each week related to daily themes. Ultimately, we'll look to the master teacher — Jesus — for guidance, bending our hearts toward His and inviting Him to teach us to pray. May the following study release an unquenchable thirst in you to know God more and encounter Him in prayer.

INTERESTED IN LEADING A GROUP?
Visit PrayingLikeJesus.com for more resources and to pick up a leader guide.

INTRODUCTION

I'm an artist. When I'm not engaged in ministry at Walnut Hill, I can be found in my studio painting or teaching art workshops. A common way to develop artistic ability is to study with a master artist for a concentrated period of time. Under the guidance of the master, a student learns the skills necessary to hone his or her craft.

This is precisely what the first disciples experienced as followers of Jesus. During His ministry on earth, Jesus invited them to travel with Him everywhere, to learn His teachings and bear witness to His life and ministry. They saw firsthand the extraordinary miracles that Jesus performed. And, as His personal entourage, they had the opportunity to ask Jesus anything they wanted.

If given the opportunity, what would you ask Jesus to teach you? I can imagine them asking a number of questions like, "Master, teach us to heal the sick." Or perhaps, "How do we raise the dead?" Maybe even, "Teach us to turn water into wine." But on one occasion, the Gospel of Luke records a disciple approaching Jesus and asking, "Lord, teach us to pray."

What caused the disciples to ask such a surprising question? Did they perceive a link between the personal prayer life of Jesus and His extraordinary power, character, teaching and ministry? They certainly saw the intimacy Jesus had with His heavenly Father, and how He lived in obedience to His voice. They watched Him retreat from large crowds to be alone in prayer — spending long periods of time there and even praying throughout the night. The disciples determined that Jesus had developed a special skill or art in prayer, and they wanted the Master Teacher to teach them this skill as well. Jesus responded by teaching His disciples what has come to be referred to as the "Lord's Prayer," because it is the prayer that He provided for His followers.

Throughout the next eight weeks, this prayer course will take you on a guided journey through the Lord's Prayer, unpacking it line by line and unearthing a treasure trove of truth based on the teachings of Jesus. It will be a safe place for you to ask questions, try new ways of connecting with God and develop your relational muscles — both with God and with each other. Along the way, we'll share some early church practices that have been used in prayer. Be advised, this is not just an academic exercise, but a very personal and interactive journey inviting you to apprentice with Jesus in learning to pray. As a result, your relationship with God will grow as you learn to pray into His will for yourself and for those around you.

So, if you are willing, along with your fellow travelers, to pray this bold prayer, then ask, "Lord, teach us to pray."

AJ PICARD
PASTOR OF PRAYER

WALNUT HILL COMMUNITY CHURCH
BETHEL, CT

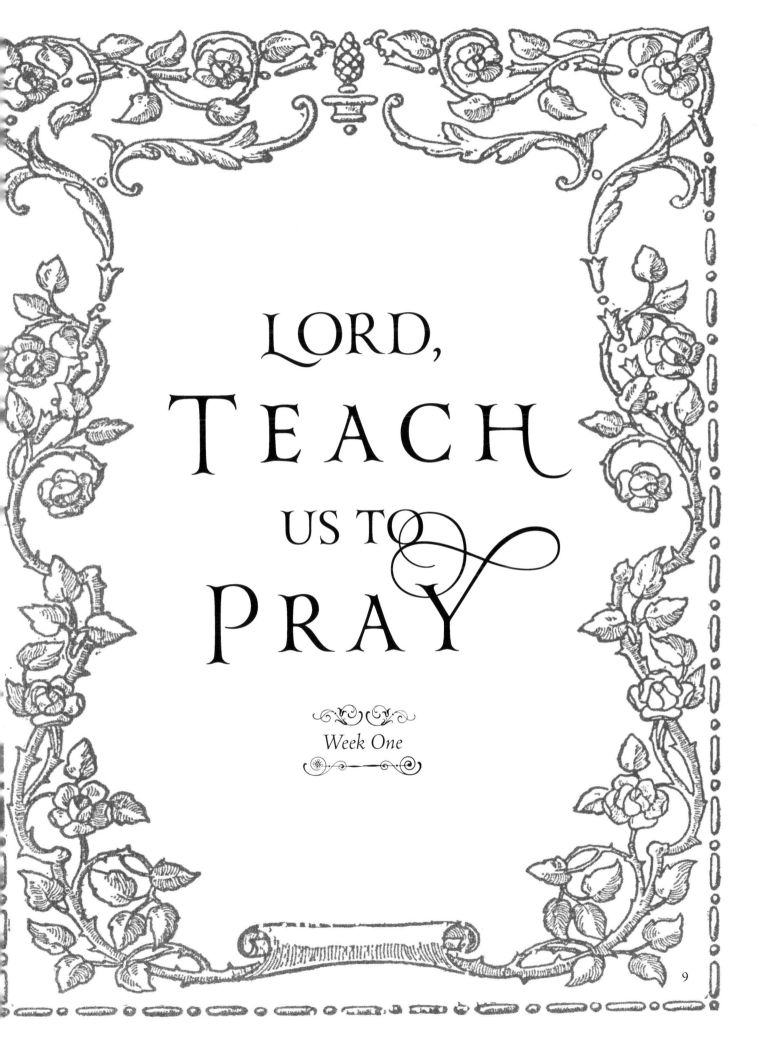

LORD, TEACH US TO PRAY

Week One

WEEK ONE

"LORD, TEACH US TO PRAY" LUKE 11:1B

Apprenticing With Jesus

"Prayer opens us to the heart of God. He is the Equipper for all whom He calls."
CHARLES STANLEY

▶◀ Watch this week's video at: www.PrayingLikeJesus.com/week-1

KEY LEARNINGS:

1. Prayer is simply _____ to God and _____ to Him.

2. How we _____ God affects how we will _____ to Him.

3. God wants you to be _____ with Him. (*Matthew 6:5*)

4. The Father wants to have a _____ relationship with you. (*Matthew 6:6*)

5. Jesus is our model for _____ with God. (*John 5:19-20a*)

6. The Lord's Prayer gives us a _____ to follow for _____ with God. (*Matthew 6:9*)

"And be sure of this: I am with you always, even to the end of the age."
MATTHEW 28:20B

"God does nothing but in answer to prayer."
JOHN WESLEY

NOTES

_____

_____

_____

_____

_____

_____

_____

_____

_____

_____

_____

_____

_____

Day 1: Getting Closer

They said to each other, "Didn't our hearts burn within us as He talked with us on the road and explained the Scriptures to us?" LUKE 24:32

It was a very cold winter in the art studio last year. In the midst of those cold harsh months, my gas heater stopped working. As I painted in a full winter coat, technicians came to uncover the problem of no heat. It was a mystery at first. The propane line was clear, electronics were all in order, and the igniter was firing, yet still … no flame. The colder the temperature dropped in my studio, the more difficult it was for the heater to start. After much trial and error, the cause of the problem was narrowed down to two small prongs on the heater spark plug. These tiny pieces of metal are positioned very close to each other so that a spark can be created between them, igniting a flame in the presence of gas. But years of prolonged use had worn down the prongs and created a subtle distance between them. As a result, the spark plug was no longer able to consistently produce a flame.

The technician did one small thing to address the problem, which had a dramatic impact on the function of the heater. He simply bent the two prongs closer together. At once, the spark ignited, producing a flame and heating the room. The simple truth was this; they just needed to get closer to one another.

It reminds me of the time when Jesus appeared to two of His disciples as they walked to Emmaus. He drew close to them, teaching them the Scriptures. As a result, their hearts burned within them. Think of it this way. You and Jesus are a bit like those two metal prongs bent toward each other, and the Holy Spirit is the flame that ignites within your heart, causing you to burn with passion for Him. You just need to get closer! This is the pivotal role of prayer in our spiritual journey.

"My secret is a very simple one: I pray," wrote Mother Teresa of Calcutta, a modern master of the skill.

> *"Prayer is simply talking to God.*
> *He speaks to us: we listen.*
> *We speak to Him: He listens.*
> *A two-way process:*
> *Speaking and listening."*
> PHILIP YANCEY ("Prayer," p. 65)

This wonderful quote from Philip Yancey is so simple yet profound. In prayer, Jesus has provided a way for us to get closer to Him so that our hearts might be warmed as our fellowship with Him grows.

DAILY JOURNAL EXERCISE

As you embark on this journey of learning to pray, may any distance that remains between you and Jesus be removed in the coming weeks as you learn the art of speaking and listening to Him, and open your heart to His great love for you.

How would you describe your relationship with God?

_____

_____

_____

Is there a small or a large distance in your heart between you and Jesus?

_____

_____

Is your heart toward God more cold, lukewarm or hot?

_____

_____

Would you like to be closer to Jesus?

_____

_____

Try talking to God about this, and ask Jesus to remove the space between you and Him in the coming weeks. Invite His Spirit to come and warm your heart as you get to know Him better.

_____

_____

_____

Day 2: Getting Real

When Jesus began to teach His disciples about prayer, He first warned them how not to pray. He said: *"And when you pray, do not be like the hypocrites, for they love to pray standing in the synagogues and on the street corners to be seen by others. Truly I tell you, they have received their reward in full."* MATTHEW 6:5 (NIV)

Jesus was confronting the spiritual leaders of His day — the Pharisees — who had made a public profession out of prayer, putting on a great outward show of their piety. He condemns their behavior as fake and calls them spiritual frauds in search of attention. Jesus continues, *"But when you pray, go into your room, close the door and pray to your Father, who is unseen. Then your Father, who sees what is done in secret, will reward you."* Matthew 6:6 (NIV)

Jesus encouraged a very different approach to prayer — one that begins in the intimate space of the home, where personal life is lived out. It wasn't that He didn't believe in public or corporate prayer. Rather, He was trying to establish authenticity in the relationship. Think of a married couple. Imagine if they only ever talked with each other in public when others were watching, but never at home. That would make the marriage relationship shallow and inauthentic, wouldn't it? For Jesus, prayer began in private — a secret place of total intimacy with God, where you could get to know Him and be known by Him. What an amazing privilege! This is where authentic prayer begins.

So, why not find your own secret place with God? It could be your favorite chair, a walk in the woods or out on the back porch. Wherever it is, your Father is waiting for you there, and your reward is to know Him personally.

DAILY JOURNAL EXERCISE

Practice getting real with God today. Set a timer for 10 minutes and be alone with God. Imagine Him sitting next to you or walking with you. What does He look like to you?

_____

_____

_____

Is your image of God kind or stern? Do you perceive God as more encouraging or critical to be with?

_____

_____

_____

What might you like to say to God? Why not tell Him about your day, and ask Him what He thought about it. Tell Him the best part of your life right now, and then tell Him the worst part. Ask God if He wants to be a part of these things. Write down His response to you. Use this time to catch up as you would with a good friend, a co-worker or your spouse. Just be real with God. This may feel awkward at first, but give it a try.

_____

_____

_____

_____

_____

Day 3: From the Heart

Jesus issues one more warning to us before He begins teaching the Lord's Prayer, *"And when you pray, do not keep on babbling like pagans, for they think they will be heard because of their many words."* MATTHEW 6:7 (NIV)

Jesus turns His attention to confronting the pagan practice of using mindless repetition in prayer — babbling on and on, using special words or magical incantations — in an attempt to get God's attention. It's the kind of prayer where your lips are moving but your heart is completely disconnected from the meaning of the words.

The truth is that many have even prayed the Lord's Prayer in this fashion, engaging in mindless recitation of words instead of thoughtful engagement with the pattern of the prayer. From the perspective of Jesus, using these prayer mantras is a kind of paganism. He says, *"Do not be like them, for your Father knows what you need before you ask Him."* Matthew 6:8 (NIV)

Jesus wants us to engage our hearts with our words instead of using mindless repetition to pray to God, who already knows our thoughts. Notice how King David expresses his heart to God in Psalm 139:1-4 (NIV), *"You have searched me, Lord, and you know me. You know when I sit and when I rise; you perceive my thoughts from afar. You discern my going out and my lying down; you are familiar with all my ways. Before a word is on my tongue you, Lord, know it completely."*

Jesus and David are in agreement that we will never bring any new information before the Lord in prayer, for He is all-knowing. Instead, we bring ourselves and our needs before the Father as His children, and connect with His heart for us. There is nothing more powerful than the bond between a parent and his or her child. Do you realize today that you have God's heart? It's true, and He's waiting to meet with you.

DAILY JOURNAL EXERCISE

Just as the disciples heard how Jesus prayed and wanted to pray like Him, it's really helpful to learn from those around us or to read the prayers recorded in Scripture to give words to our own prayers. Prayer is caught more than taught. Read Psalm 139, a prayer of David, allowing these words to become your own prayer to God. If it helps you, read it out loud. Journal about this experience, describing what stands out to you in this very honest and heartfelt prayer.

Psalm 139

O LORD, you have examined my heart and know everything about me.
You know when I sit down or stand up. You know my thoughts even when I'm far away.
You see me when I travel and when I rest at home. You know everything I do.
You know what I am going to say even before I say it, LORD.
You go before me and follow me. You place your hand of blessing on my head.
Such knowledge is too wonderful for me, too great for me to understand!

I can never escape from your Spirit! I can never get away from your presence!
If I go up to Heaven, you are there; if I go down to the grave, you are there.
If I ride the wings of the morning, if I dwell by the farthest oceans,
even there your hand will guide me, and your strength will support me.
I could ask the darkness to hide me and the light around me to become night —
but even in darkness I cannot hide from you.
To you the night shines as bright as day. Darkness and light are the same to you.

You made all the delicate, inner parts of my body and knit me together in my mother's womb.
Thank you for making me so wonderfully complex! Your workmanship is marvelous—how well I know it.
You watched me as I was being formed in utter seclusion, as I was woven together in the dark of the womb.
You saw me before I was born. Every day of my life was recorded in your book.
Every moment was laid out before a single day had passed.

How precious are your thoughts about me, O God. They cannot be numbered!
I can't even count them; they outnumber the grains of sand!
And when I wake up, you are still with me!

O God, if only you would destroy the wicked! Get out of my life, you murderers!
They blaspheme you; your enemies misuse your name.
O LORD, shouldn't I hate those who hate you? Shouldn't I despise those who oppose you?
Yes, I hate them with total hatred, for your enemies are my enemies.

Search me, O God, and know my heart; test me and know my anxious thoughts.
Point out anything in me that offends you, and lead me along the path of everlasting life.

Day 4:
It's All About Jesus

The essence of prayer is relationship with God, and Jesus showed us how to live in relationship with His Father when He was here on earth.

The essence of prayer is relationship with God, and Jesus showed us how to live in relationship with His Father when He was here on earth. He explained, *"I tell you the truth, the Son can do nothing by Himself. He does only what He sees the Father doing. Whatever the Father does, the Son also does. For the Father loves the Son and shows Him everything He is doing." John 5:19-20a*

Here Jesus reveals a relational model of living for us to follow. He expresses total dependence on the Father for strength, guidance and direction. But how did Jesus receive this direction from His Father? Luke 5:16 (NIV) tells us, *"Jesus often withdrew to lonely places and prayed."* On one occasion, after large crowds pursued Jesus to hear Him preach and watch Him heal the sick, we learn that, *"Very early in the morning, while it was still dark, Jesus got up, left the house and went off to a solitary place, where He prayed." Mark 1:35 (NIV)*

Relationships require time set apart to listen and share. The same is true in our prayer lives. There was great activity before and after Jesus' solitary times of prayer, but do you ever wonder what happened during them? We are given a glimpse into a personal prayer encounter when Jesus went to an olive grove called Gethsemane to pour out His heart before the Father.

"He (Jesus) went on a little farther and bowed with His face to the ground, praying, 'My Father! If it is possible, let this cup of suffering be taken away from me. Yet I want your will to be done, not mine.'" Matthew 26:39

What can you learn about Jesus' relationship with the Father from this passage?

_____

_____

_____

In this relational model, who was leading? Who was following?

_____

_____

_____

It's encouraging to know that even Jesus needed some space to be alone with His Father to get connected, feel His love, and submit to His will and purpose. Before we unpack the pattern of prayer that Jesus teaches His disciples, let's pay special attention to the lifestyle Jesus reveals to us. It's all about Jesus, and He's the ultimate model for relationship with God.

DAILY JOURNAL EXERCISE

At this early stage in our journey, it can be very powerful to receive a blessing from those who have gone before us in prayer. The apostle Paul had a deep and rich relationship with God that he poured out into the lives of others. For today's exercise, read Ephesians 3:14-21 and allow yourself to receive Paul's prayer for spiritual growth as if he were speaking it to your own heart. Soak in the words of this prayer, and let your spirit say yes to Paul's invitation to encounter more of God.

A Prayer for Spiritual Growth

"When I think of all this, I fall to my knees and pray to the Father, the Creator of everything in Heaven and on earth. I pray that from His glorious, unlimited resources He will empower you with inner strength through His Spirit. Then Christ will make His home in your hearts as you trust in Him. Your roots will grow down into God's love and keep you strong. And may you have the power to understand, as all God's people should, how wide, how long, how high, and how deep His love is. May you experience the love of Christ, though it is too great to understand fully. Then you will be made complete with all the fullness of life and power that comes from God.

"Now all glory to God, who is able, through His mighty power at work within us, to accomplish infinitely more than we might ask or think. Glory to Him in the church and in Christ Jesus through all generations forever and ever! Amen." EPHESIANS 3:14-21

_____

_____

_____

_____

_____

_____

_____

_____

Day 5: A Model Prayer

The disciples have sought out the Master Teacher for guidance in prayer. In response, Jesus issued a few initial words of warning. Now, He presents His apprentices with the greatest prayer ever conceived or imagined.

Authored by Jesus Himself, inspired by the Holy Spirit and perfectly worded, it is a model for prayer. When Jesus revealed the Lord's Prayer to His disciples, He did not say, "Pray this," but rather, *"Pray like this"* (Matthew 6:9). He intended to give the disciples an example to follow — a pattern for Christian communion with God — so that repetition might lead to rich appreciation and learning.

In this pattern of prayer, it is clear to whom we are speaking. We are approaching the King of kings, and Lord of lords, the sovereign Creator and Ruler of the universe. It is no small thing to be in conversation with God Himself. How amazing to be invited into this privileged relationship! And we ought to remember who we are. We are not God. Rather, we are the created speaking to our Creator. How awesome and humbling this is to consider.

Jesus invites us to learn how to pray into the will of God by following a pattern, one that has a lot of references to "Your" – "Your name … Your Kingdom … Your will." The use of "us" comes later, and this is by design. We discover that God's list comes first, and our list comes second. This is good, as it exalts God's concerns over our own. He *is* God, after all.

> *"This, then, is how you should pray:*
> '*Our Father in Heaven, hallowed be Your name,*
> *Your Kingdom come, Your will be done, on earth as it is in Heaven.*
> *Give us today our daily bread.*
> *And forgive us our debts, as we also have forgiven our debtors.*
> *And lead us not into temptation, but deliver us from the evil one.*
> *[For yours is the Kingdom and the power and the glory forever. Amen.]**'"
> ** found in some manuscripts though not all.*
> *Matthew 6:9-13 (NIV)*

DAILY JOURNAL EXERCISE

What do you think about when you hear the Lord's Prayer? Do you have any memories of it from your own experiences? Are they positive or negative experiences?

_____

_____

Now think about your own prayer life. Would you say it's more of a "laundry list" of your needs?

_____

_____

Take a moment to reflect and write out a description of a typical prayer that you might pray.

_____

_____

_____

If you were to create a "model" out of your prayer, what might it look like?

_____

_____

_____

Now begin to ask God how this prayer should change in the coming weeks.

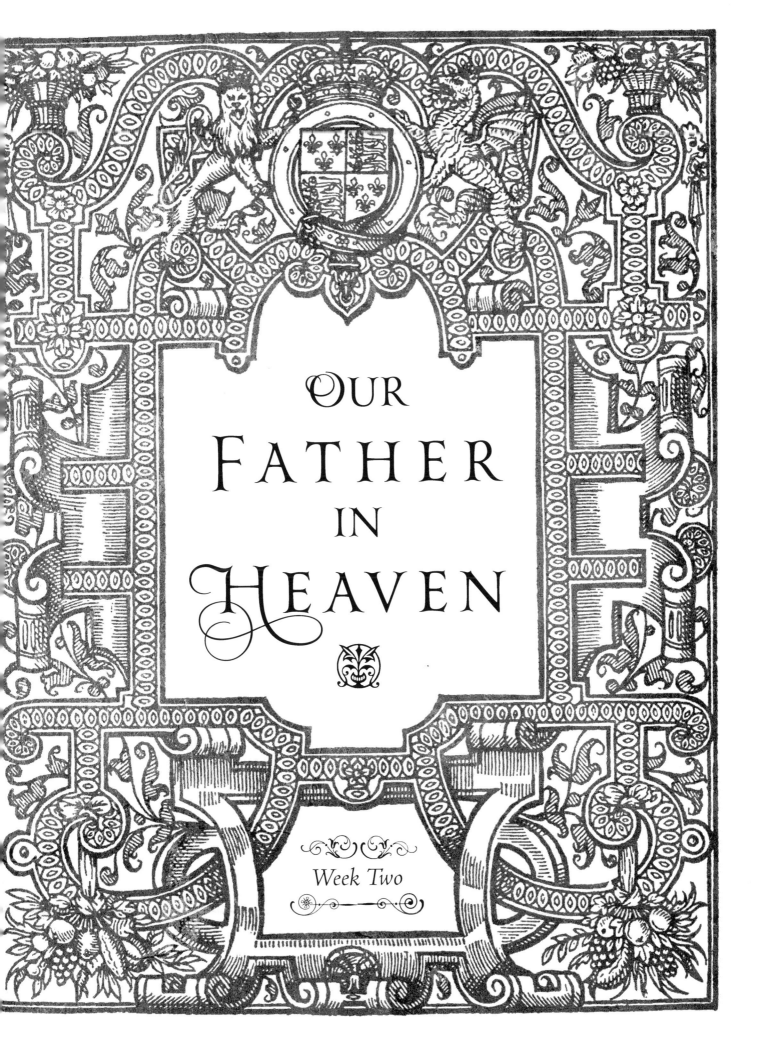

OUR FATHER IN HEAVEN

Week Two

WEEK TWO

"OUR FATHER IN HEAVEN..." MATTHEW 6:9

Intimacy With God

"For prayer is nothing else than being on terms of friendship with God."
SAINT TERESA OF AVILA

Watch this week's video at: www.PrayingLikeJesus.com/week-2

KEY LEARNINGS:

1. We were created in the _____ of God. *(Genesis 1:26-27)*

2. We were created for _____ with God. *(Genesis 3:8a, Colossians 1:16)*

3. Through Jesus, we become part of God's _____. *(Galatians 4:4-7)*

4. Our heavenly Father is _____. *(James 1:17)*

5. We are _____ by God, and we _____ to Him. *(1 Peter 2:9-10)*

"Intimacy with God – His highest priority for our lives – determines the impact of our lives."
CHARLES STANLEY

NOTES

Day 1: Hardwired for Relationship

Our willingness to be in relationship with our Father has a lot to do with how we perceive His character. Does God actually care about us? Is He mad at us? Can we trust Him?

It is entirely possible that our view of God is affecting our willingness to draw near to Him in prayer. Let's take a look at God's original intention for us as human beings in the beginning:

- Genesis 1:26-27: *"Then God said, 'Let us make human beings in our image, to be like us (emphasis added)' … So God created human beings in His own image, in the image of God He created them; male and female He created them."* Scripture reveals God the Father, Son and Holy Spirit as "triune." The three-in-one God is relational in nature, creating us out of perfect fellowship. The implication is that we have been hardwired for relationship. Made in the image of God, it's in our nature to want to connect with Him. This is by design, for the Creator of the heavens and the earth created us for relationship with Him.

- Genesis 2:8-9a (NIV): *Now the LORD God had planted a garden in the east, in Eden; and there He put the man he had formed. And the LORD God made all kinds of trees grow out of the ground — trees that were pleasing to the eye and good for food."* God's intentions toward us were good! He created a beautiful garden for man and woman to live in. This was God's dwelling place with Adam and Eve, a place of intimate fellowship with them.

- Genesis 2:19 (NIV): *"Now the LORD God had formed out of the ground all the wild animals and all the birds in the sky. He brought them to the man to see what he would name them; and whatever the man called each living creature, that was its name …"* God empowers Adam to collaborate with Him! He spent time with Adam naming each animal. He could have named them Himself, but instead chose to do it with Adam, one by one. It was a partnership in which God enjoyed collaborating with Adam.

- Genesis 3:8a (NIV): *"Then the man and his wife heard the sound of the LORD God as He was walking in the garden in the cool of the day …"* Scripture reveals that God even walked in the garden in the cool of the day. He was present with us, spending time with us.

DAILY JOURNAL EXERCISE

As you read the Genesis story, it's amazing to see how close God walked with Adam. Do you believe that God wants to be in relationship with you? If not, write down why.

_____

_____

_____

_____

Why not ask God if He wants to be in relationship with you?

_____

_____

Do you believe you were made in the image of God? How do you think that impacts your value?

_____

_____

_____

In what ways are you best reflecting God's character?

_____

_____

_____

_____

Day 2: Sons & Daughters

The first two words Jesus taught His disciples to pray, "Our Father," were quite shocking.

As Jews, they had many names for God up to this point. He was Yahweh — "I AM WHO I AM." He was Jehovah-Elohim (the Eternal Creator), El-Elyon (the Lord Most High) and Jehovah-Shalom (the Lord our Peace) — just to name a few. Now, Jesus invites His disciples to pray to God as "Abba."

"Abba" is an Aramaic word, one that is uttered from the lips of infants, revealing their instinctive trust in "daddy" to care for their needs. This word is so intimate, revealing God as very close to us, not far off. And if God is "our" Father, then we are His children, part of a family filled with brothers and sisters. How is this so?

In John 5:19-20a, Jesus expresses His dependence on the Father as the Son of God. He says, *"I tell you the truth, the Son can do nothing by Himself. He does only what He sees the Father doing. Whatever the Father does, the Son also does. For the Father loves the Son and shows Him everything He is doing."* Jesus models intimacy with God and obedience to His Father during His earthly ministry. Then He instructs His disciples to do the same. In John 14:6, Jesus says, *"I am the way, the truth, and the life. No one can come to the Father except through me."*

This is a declaration that our identity is rooted in Christ alone. Our access to the Father comes through surrender to Jesus. We've been adopted into God's family, a diverse community of sons and daughters who share the same heavenly Father through faith in Christ. Isn't it wonderful to know that you are not alone, but part of God's family?!

DAILY JOURNAL EXERCISE

Read Galatians 4:4-7:

"But when the right time came, God sent His Son, born of a woman, subject to the law. God sent Him to buy freedom for us who were slaves to the law, so that He could adopt us as His very own children. And because we are his children, God has sent the Spirit of His Son into our hearts, prompting us to call out, "Abba, Father." Now you are no longer a slave but God's own child. And since you are His child, God has made you His heir."

Not only does the Son give us the right to address God as our Father, but the Holy Spirit, assisting us in our prayer lives, prompts us to cry out, "Abba, Father!"

Do you believe that you are a son or daughter of God?

_____

What is the significance of realizing our adoption into God's family when we pray?

_____

_____

Spend some time talking with your heavenly Father. If you have never called Him Father, start by telling Him why, or what your thoughts are about Him. Try asking your Father specific questions. Come up with your own or use the ones below:

+ When you look at me, what do you see?

+ Father, what is your favorite thing about me?

+ Father, are you proud of me?

_____

_____

_____

_____

Day 3: Changing Your Perspective

When our Lord Jesus designed the invocation to His prayer, "Our Father in Heaven," He set out to reveal both the extraordinary love and concern of a Father for His children, set amid the expansive vision of an eternal, infinite and almighty God.

He is a perfect Father, unchanging and unlimited in His capacity to respond to the needs that we bring to Him.

This perspective of God puts us in our place. We are humbled, but not in a way that makes us feel unimportant or insignificant before Him. Instead, we ponder, "He's my Father, but He is God in Heaven! He's God in Heaven, yet He bends down to love me as His child! It's unimaginable but it's true!" And as this truth takes hold of us, we are lifted to greater heights of awe and wonder at the majesty of our loving God. This is a Father worthy of our respect and reverence.

- Paul describes Him as, *"the God who made the world and everything in it. Since He is Lord of Heaven and earth, He doesn't live in man-made temples, and human hands can't serve His needs …" Acts 17:24-25a*

- The prophet Isaiah declared, *"The high and lofty one who lives in eternity, the Holy One, says this: 'I live in the high and holy place with those whose spirits are contrite and humble …'" Isaiah 57:15*

- Job said, *"We cannot imagine the power of the Almighty; but even though He is just and righteous, He does not destroy us." Job 37:23*

This vision of God leads us to pray with great admiration and devotion.

DAILY JOURNAL EXERCISE

Can you think of any ways that the majesty of God is shown around us?

_____

_____

How often do you pause to take note of the greatness of God?

_____

_____

What response should an awareness of God's majesty draw out of us?

_____

_____

Practice writing a letter to God, telling Him how wonderful He is.

_____

_____

_____

_____

_____

_____

_____

Day 4: Renewing Your Father Image

"Every good and perfect gift is from above, coming down from the Father of the heavenly lights, who does not change like shifting shadows." JAMES 1:17 (NIV)

Our earthly fathers were meant to model, reflect and reveal many of the characteristics of our heavenly Father. But for many of us, that was far from the case. Take some time to reflect on your earthly father and describe his qualities.

How was your relationship with him?

_____

_____

How might this have shaped your ideas of your heavenly Father?

_____

_____

In what ways do their character line up?

_____

_____

Thank God for these similarities of character. How might they differ?

_____

_____

Ask God to reveal more of His nature to you, so that you can experience how good, loving and dependable He is.

DAILY JOURNAL EXERCISE

Read this list of a selection of God's attributes as revealed in Scripture. As you do, invite your heavenly Father to renew your image of Him.

What is your heavenly Father like?

> *He is patient: His anger lasts only a moment, but His favor lasts a lifetime. (Psalm 30:5a)*
>
> *He is compassionate, slow to anger, and abounding in love and faithfulness. (Exodus 34:6)*
>
> *He is joyful, kind, gentle and humble.*
> *(Nehemiah 8:10, Matthew 11:29, Romans 2:4, 2 Corinthians 10:1, Galatians 5:22-23)*
>
> *He is the giver of good gifts. (James 1:17, Psalms 84:11)*
>
> *He is the same yesterday and today and forever. (Hebrews 13:8)*
>
> *He is good. (Psalm 100:5)*
>
> *He is holy. (1 Samuel 2:2, Joshua 24:19)*
>
> *He is the source of hope. (Jeremiah 29:11)*
>
> *He is the source of peace. (John 14:27)*
>
> *He is caring. (1 Peter 5:7)*
>
> *He is trusting. (Ephesians 2:10)*
>
> *He gives rest. (Matthew 11:28)*
>
> *He is near to all who call on Him. (Psalm 145:18)*
>
> *He is the one who is close to the brokenhearted. (Psalm 34:18)*
>
> *He is our protector. (Psalm 32:7)*
>
> *He is our fortress, help and hiding place. (2 Samuel 22:2; Psalm 40:17; Psalm 32:7)*
>
> *He is righteous and just. (Psalm 89:14, Psalm 111:7)*
>
> *He is the everlasting King! (Jeremiah 10:10)*

Which of God's attributes resonates with you as true to God's character?

_____

_____

Which ones are more difficult for you to believe?

_____

_____

Ask God why that might be. Invite Him to change your view of Him in these areas.

_____

Day 5: Knowing Who You Are

"… For you are a chosen people. You are royal priests, a holy nation, God's very own possession. As a result, you can show others the goodness of God, for He called you out of the darkness into His wonderful light. Once you had no identity as a people; now you are God's people." 1 PETER 2:9-10A

Yesterday, we addressed the need to renew our image of God the Father. Today, we'll turn the mirror inward on ourselves. Wrong perceptions of ourselves can be the most difficult to combat. As human beings, it's almost impossible to behave in a manner that is inconsistent with how we see ourselves. Feelings of rejection, shame, guilt, low self-worth, fear and anxiety all seek to undermine our true identity in Christ. We must know who we are to let our actions agree with our true identity.

Our relationship with God — in Christ — is the cornerstone of our identity as followers of Jesus. In today's Scripture passage, we find a clear declaration that informs us of who we are in Christ:

+ **We are a chosen people.** We belong to God our Father, standing with our brothers and sisters in Christ.

+ **We are royal priests.** We have great significance in ministry, serving King Jesus.

+ **We are a holy nation.** We are a family set apart for the purposes of God and purified by Christ. His character is alive in us.

+ **We are God's very own possession.** We are safe and secure under His care.

Our identity in Jesus gives us a deep sense of security, significance and belonging as we live in the light of God's love. Jesus said in John 8:32, *"And you will know the truth, and the truth will set you free."* The truth is that we are safe and secure in Him. Allow this revelation of your true identity to reveal any wrong perceptions you may be struggling with, so that the truth of who you are will set you free.

DAILY JOURNAL EXERCISE

Who I am in Christ: Meditate on the truth of who you are in Christ as revealed in Scripture.

I am Accepted in Christ

John 1:12	I am God's child.
John 15:5	I am Christ's friend.
Romans 5:1	I have been justified.
1 Corinthians 6:17	I am united with the Lord and one with Him in spirit.
1 Corinthians 6:19-20	I have been bought with a price: I belong to God.
1 Corinthians 12:27	I am a member of Christ's body.
Ephesians 1:1	I am a saint, a holy one.
Ephesians 1:5	I have been adopted as God's child.
Ephesians 2:18	I have direct access to God through the Holy Spirit.
Colossians 1:14	I have been redeemed and forgiven of all my sins.
Colossians 2:10	I am complete in Christ.

I am Secure in Christ

Romans 8:1-2	I am free from condemnation.
Romans 8:28	I am assured that all things work together for good.
Romans 8:31-34	I am free from any condemning charges against me.
Romans 8:35-39	I cannot be separated from the love of God.
2 Corinthians 1:21-22	I have been established, anointed and sealed by God.
Colossians 3:3	I am hidden with Christ in God.
Philippians 1:6	I am confident that the good work God has begun in me will be perfected.
Philippians 3:20	I am a citizen of Heaven.
2 Timothy 1:7	I have not been given a spirit of fear, but of power, love and discipline.
Hebrews 4:16	I can find grace and mercy in time of need.
1 John 5:18	I am born of God, and the evil one cannot touch me.

I am Significant in Christ

Matthew 5:13-14	I am the salt of the earth and the light of the world.
John 15:1,5	I am a branch of the true vine, Jesus, a channel of His life.
John 15:16	I have been chosen and appointed to bear fruit.
Acts 1:8	I am a personal, Spirit-empowered witness of Christ.
1 Corinthians 3:16	I am a temple of God.
2 Corinthians 5:17-21	I am a minister of reconciliation for God.
2 Corinthians 6:1	I am God's co-worker.
Ephesians 2:6	I am seated with Christ in the heavenly realm.
Ephesians 2:10	I am God's workmanship, created for good works.
Ephesians 3:12	I may approach God with freedom and confidence.
Philippians 4:13	I can do all things through Christ who strengthens me!

(ADAPTED FROM "RESTORED," BY NEIL ANDERSON, PP.153-155)

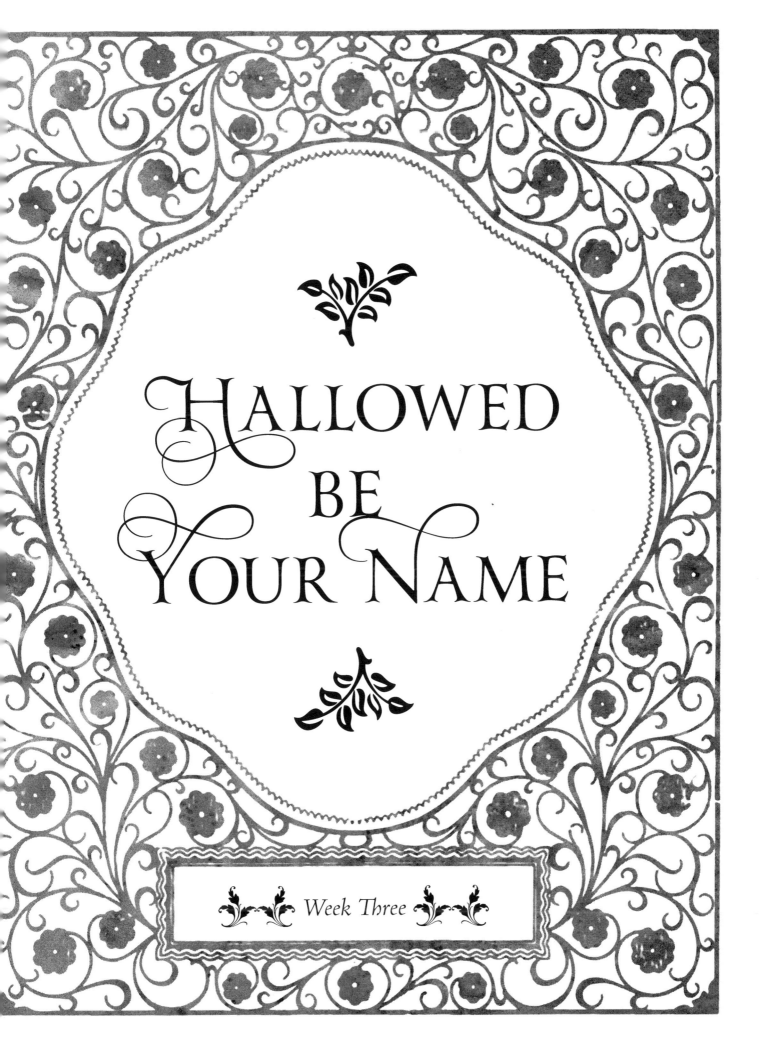

WEEK THREE

"HALLOWED BE YOUR NAME" MATTHEW 6:9 (NIV)

Adoration and Praise

"I believe that the greatest form of prayer is praise to God."
BILLY GRAHAM

▶◀ Watch this week's video at: www.PrayingLikeJesus.com/week-3

KEY LEARNINGS:

1. God's name is significant in revealing His _____ and _____. *(Exodus 3:13-15)*

2. Using Scripture is a powerful way to _____ your prayers of _____.

3. Praise is a language of _____, called _____.

4. As we _____ the Lord, we become _____ Him. *(2 Corinthians 3:16-18)*

5. Time spent in God's _____ transforms our lives. *(Exodus 33:11)*

"Our emotions are made by God, and these too must bow down before Him."
LAURA STORY

NOTES

_____

_____

_____

_____

_____

_____

_____

_____

_____

_____

_____

_____

_____

Day 1: Worship of the King

"Not to us, LORD, not to us, but to your name be the glory." PSALM 115:1 (NIV)

We've discovered how personal a relationship with our heavenly Father can be. Now it's time to pause and worship Him for who He is.

Jesus, in teaching us to pray, calls us to hold the name of God in high esteem. "Hallowed be your name" can also be translated "may your name be kept holy." This is both a plea and a pledge to praise the name of God. It's a plea that we would enter into God's presence every day with a fresh awareness of His power and majesty. It's also a pledge to seek God's face before we ever seek His hand. "Hallowed be Your name" is a prayer of praise, where we seek His face by focusing our attention on God's divine nature — His character and attributes.

J. I. Packer explains, "'Hallowed' means known, acknowledged, and honored as holy. 'Holy' is the Bible word for all that makes God different from us, in particular His awesome power and purity." (J. I. Packer, "Praying the Lord's Prayer," p. 42)

Our God is holy. Unlike us, His thoughts are pure, His intentions are good, His love is boundless, His ways are true, His plan is perfect, His compassion is constant, His authority is ultimate, His resources are limitless, His face is radiant, and His faithfulness is endless. He is a God worthy of our worship! Let's join with the psalmist and pray, *"Not to us, LORD, … but to your name be the glory."*

DAILY JOURNAL EXERCISE

In your own words, what does it mean to hallow God's name?

_____

_____

What might it look like for you to keep God's name holy in your life?

_____

_____

How does it glorify God to focus on Him first before ourselves?

_____

_____

Do you think you might pray differently after worshipping God for who He is?

_____

_____

_____

_____

DAY 2: MAGNIFY

"Oh, magnify the LORD with me, and let us exalt His name together!"
PSALM 34:3 (ESV)

Magnify — *verb.* To make (something) greater; to enlarge in appearance.

There are many types of lenses designed to magnify an object, such as telescopes, microscopes, binoculars and telephoto lenses. Interestingly, the object doesn't change at all, yet the perspective of the viewer is changed dramatically when peering through the lens. Scientists place organisms under microscopes to study their cellular makeup, and stargazers peer through telescopes to marvel at far off constellations.

The enemy desires for us to magnify our worries, zooming in on anxious thoughts and bringing them into sharp focus. This is how fear, uncertainty and doubt are empowered as giants in our lives, hindering our relationship with God. The answer lies in a change of perspective.

Many of us, if we are honest, would acknowledge that we need a healed view of God. Instead of staring at our problems, let's magnify the Lord, and focus on His eternal character and nature. Zoom in on His goodness, compassion and love. Meditate on His mighty power displayed throughout Scripture. Become so enamored of Jesus that our confidence is established in the awareness of **who He is** and **who we are in Him.**

Hebrews 11:1 (NIV) says, *"Now faith is confidence in what we hope for and assurance about what we do not see."* This assurance is built on knowing who God is and enlarging our view of Him in the midst of our circumstances. By faith, we are empowered to walk through the storm with our eyes fixed on our overcoming King. We worship the Lord in advance for the way He will bring us through the storm. So, get out your telescopes, look to the heavens and magnify the Lord!

DAILY JOURNAL EXERCISE

It's so encouraging to know that, when we lack the inspiration to express our own praise to God, all we need to do is pick up the Psalms and join our hearts with the words of Scripture. Using Scripture as our guide is a powerful way of equipping our prayers of praise by magnifying the Lord. Practice honoring God's name by reading Psalm 23 and listing the unique attributes of God that are revealed in this Psalm.

Psalm 23

A PSALM OF DAVID

The LORD is my shepherd;
I have all that I need.
He lets me rest in green meadows;
He leads me beside peaceful streams.
He renews my strength.
He guides me along right paths,
bringing honor to His name.
Even when I walk
through the darkest valley,
I will not be afraid,

for You are close beside me.
Your rod and your staff
protect and comfort me.
You prepare a feast for me
in the presence of my enemies.
You honor me by anointing my head with oil.
My cup overflows with blessings.
Surely Your goodness and unfailing love will pursue me all the days of my life,
and I will live in the house of the LORD forever.

_____

_____

_____

_____

_____

Day 3: What's in a Name?

"Ascribe to the LORD the glory due His name." PSALM 29:2 (NIV)

The Father's name is extremely important to Jesus, as it is tied to both His identity and reputation. In fact, the word "name" actually means "identity" in Aramaic. God identifies Himself with many different names in the Bible to reveal His character. Here are two significant moments:

"When Abram was ninety-nine years old, the LORD appeared to him and said, 'I am El-Shaddai — God Almighty.'" Genesis 17:1a

When God called Moses to lead His people out of Egypt, he protested saying,

"If I go to the people of Israel and tell them, 'The God of your ancestors has sent me to you,' they will ask me, 'What is his name?' Then what should I tell them?

"God replied to Moses, 'I Am Who I Am. Say this to the people of Israel: I Am has sent me to you.' God also said to Moses, 'Say this to the people of Israel: Yahweh, the God of your ancestors — the God of Abraham, the God of Isaac, and the God of Jacob — has sent me to you. This is my eternal name, my name to remember for all generations.'" Exodus 3:13-15

We learn from this passage that Yahweh is the eternal name of God, meaning "I Am Who I Am." This name conveys that:

- **God is eternal:** He existed before time began, and operates outside of time.

- **God is constant and unchanging:** Before we ever were, He IS.

- **God is unshakable:** His identity is not influenced by our perceptions of Him.

Elizabeth Browning penned the famous line, *"How do I love thee? Let me count the ways …"* When we look at the prayer life of King David, we see this love struck bias toward the qualities of his beloved God. The Psalms of David overflow with expressions of adoration and praise:

- *"Come, let us tell of the Lord's greatness; let us exalt His name together." Psalm 34:3*

- *"Let them praise your great and awesome name. Your name is holy!" Psalm 99:3*

- *"Exalt the Lord our God! Bow low before His feet, for He is holy!" Psalm 99:5*

DAILY JOURNAL EXERCISE

Honoring God's name: The Bible provides countless descriptions of God's nature for us to explore. As you read through Scripture, look for words that describe who God is to you, and begin to develop your own "ABC's of Adoration." Try going through the alphabet using each letter as a name for God.

Example:

+ **Abba** You are my Father.

+ **Beloved** You are my dearly loved God

+ **Creator** You are the maker of the universe.

+

+

+

+

+

+

+

+

+

+

+

+

+

+

+

+

+

+

+

Day 4:
A King After God's Own Heart

King David was a man after God's heart. On one occasion, he praised the Lord in the presence of the whole assembly of Israel.

"O Lord, the God of our ancestor Israel, may You be praised forever and ever! Yours, O Lord, is the greatness, the power, the glory, the victory, and the majesty. Everything in the heavens and on earth is yours, O Lord, and this is your Kingdom. We adore you as the one who is over all things. Wealth and honor come from you alone, for you rule over everything. Power and might are in your hand, and at your discretion people are made great and given strength. O our God, we thank you and praise your glorious name!"
1 Chronicles 29:10-13

How powerful to see the King of Israel publicly acknowledging that the kingdom belongs to God. Notice how David focused on God's divine attributes in this prayer. He begins by listing God's virtues: His greatness, power, glory, victory and majesty. David pours out his adoration before God, much like someone in love describes the qualities of his or her beloved.

Praise is an act of adoration. It is a language of love. As you adore God and focus on the attributes you love about Him, you are agreeing with the truth of who God is and appropriating His goodness into

your own life through prayer. This focus on God's divine nature begins to transform your own nature in the process.

David says in Psalm 27:4 (NIV), *"One thing I ask from the LORD, this only do I seek: that I may dwell in the house of the LORD all the days of my life, to gaze on the beauty of the LORD and to seek Him in His temple."* (Emphasis added.)

David's focus is riveted on the Lord. When we focus our attention on *who God is*, and "gaze on His beauty," we become captivated by Him. In this process, our perspective changes, our faith expands, our hearts grow, our joy increases, and we are transformed!

DAILY JOURNAL EXERCISE

Reflecting on your own life, would people around you know who you adore?

_____

What are your favorite things about God?

_____

_____

What qualities does God possess that you long to develop in your own life?

_____

_____

Take a walk outside with God this week. Begin to praise Him as you see things in creation. Use all your senses to connect with God. As you hear, smell and feel, talk to God about who He is to you. Make a note of what you experienced with God.

_____

_____

_____

_____

Day 5:
Face to Face

"Inside the Tent of Meeting, the LORD would speak to Moses face to face, as one speaks to a friend. Afterward, Moses would return to the camp, but the young man who assisted him, Joshua son of Nun, would remain behind in the Tent of Meeting." EXODUS 33:11

Let's take a moment to reflect on another great hero in Scripture, the mighty warrior Joshua. We know how closely his mentor, Moses, walked with God, but young Joshua intrigues me. I've often wondered what caused Joshua to have such courage in the face of adversity. How could he confront a culture of fear, yet remain focused on God's promises instead of becoming paralyzed by enemy armies and oversized giants while leading Israel into battle? Was Joshua born with some unusual capacity to believe, or was it something he developed in his relationship with God? I believe it was the latter.

In Exodus 33:11, we catch a glimpse of Joshua — almost as an addendum to the text — revealing his early exposure to the presence of God. As the young assistant to Moses, Joshua was there in the Tent of Meeting when Moses would speak to God face to face. Joshua encountered God's tangible presence, and he wanted more. It says right there at the end of verse 11 that, when Moses left, Joshua would remain.

What would happen if we frequently spent time face to face with God, enjoying His presence? As we focus on His goodness revealed in Scripture, our vision of Him becomes so big that our current crisis pales in comparison to His promises to us. I have come to the conclusion that Joshua moved ahead by remaining behind. When he lingered with the Lord, he encountered God's goodness — after which, no giant could stand a chance.

DAILY JOURNAL EXERCISE

But whenever someone turns to the Lord, the veil is taken away. For the Lord is the Spirit, and wherever the Spirit of the Lord is, there is freedom. So all of us who have had that veil removed can see and reflect the glory of the Lord. And the Lord — who is the Spirit — makes us more and more like Him as we are changed into His glorious image." 2 Corinthians 3:16-18

Face-to-face encounters with God have not been relegated to Old Covenant experiences that only men like Moses and Joshua could enjoy because of their unique callings. A reading of 2 Corinthians Chapter 3 reveals that, under the New Covenant in Christ, God's presence lives within us by His Spirit.

Put on some worship music that you enjoy, and begin to focus on God's presence. Spend 15 minutes just worshiping God, focusing on His presence and declaring your love for Him. Enjoy His presence as you let God's Spirit minister to you.

Your
KINGDOM
COME

Your Will be Done

ON EARTH
AS IT IS IN
HEAVEN

Week Four

WEEK FOUR

"YOUR KINGDOM COME, YOUR WILL BE DONE ON EARTH AS IT IS IN HEAVEN." MATTHEW 6:10 (NIV)

Intercession and Listening to God's Voice

"Intercession is putting yourself in God's place; it is having His mind and His perspective."
OSWALD CHAMBERS

▶◀ Watch this week's video at: www.PrayingLikeJesus.com/week-4

KEY LEARNINGS:

1. The Kingdom of God is the realm of God's _____, where people _____ their lives to Him. *(Mark 1:15)*

2. Satan led humankind away from _____ with God. Our _____ to rule was transferred to him when we rebelled. *(Genesis 3:4-7, Ephesians 2:2)*

3. Jesus came to _____ the Kingdom of God on earth. He took back _____ of this world. *(Colossians 1:13-14)*

4. God has a _____. God wants us to participate in His _____. *(1 John 5:14)*

5. Jesus learned God's will by _____ _____ with Him. Jesus regularly spent time _____ with God in _____. *(Luke 5:16)*

6. God wants to speak to us through _____ _____. *(2 Timothy 3:16)*

"The hinge of history is the bended knee."
PETE GREIG

"The task of every generation is to discover in which direction the Sovereign Redeemer is going, then move in that direction."
JONATHAN EDWARDS

NOTES

DAY 1: SURRENDER

"The time has come ... The Kingdom of God has come near. Repent and believe the good news!" MARK 1:15 (NIV)

Our natural tendency is to start with our own prayer list — our needs, our requests and our desires. But Jesus taught us to pray, "Your Kingdom come." In doing so, He shifts our focus away from ourselves to God's prayer list: His will, His plans and His desires for us and for humanity. But where is God's Kingdom to be found, and how do we identify its presence?

A CHANGE OF ALLEGIANCE: The Kingdom of God, simply put, is the realm of God's domain. This is not a place you go, but a relationship you have. It exists where people relinquish control of their lives to Jesus, surrendering to Him as King. The good news is that He's not a tyrant but a servant. Our King rules not as a dictator but a shepherd.

Jesus came to earth as the Son of God to die and rise again so that we could be forgiven and restored to a right, loving relationship with our Father. When we repent and follow Jesus, we acknowledge our rebellion, saying we're sorry for the ways we've sinned and asking forgiveness. This change of allegiance calls us out of darkness and into the light. Then God sends us the Holy Spirit to live in us, helping us to live in a new way. Imagine, the God of Heaven coming to live in the hearts and lives of His people!

This is the rule of the ungrieved, unquenched Holy Spirit within us. As the Spirit is given reign, we become a gateway for the Kingdom of Heaven to come to earth. Praying "Your Kingdom come" invites God to pour His Spirit in and through us so that we can carry out His Kingdom here on earth. As citizens of Heaven and subjects of the King, we usher in God's Kingdom through our surrendered lives.

DAILY JOURNAL EXERCISE

When you hear the word "surrender," what image comes to mind? Is this a positive or negative image?

_____

_____

What makes it difficult to put God's Kingdom before your own?

_____

_____

Is Jesus inviting you to surrender anything today so that His Kingdom will be first in your life? Allow God to speak to you about this.

_____

_____

_____

Have you surrendered your life to Jesus? If not, you can do it right now by saying you're sorry for your sin, believe that Jesus is Lord, and surrender your life to Him in prayer. Then invite the Holy Spirit to come live in you.*

_____

_____

_____

*If you have done this for the first time, tell someone! We would love to celebrate with you and help you to grow in your faith._

DAY 2: THE KINGDOM RESTORED

To understand God's plan of restoration, let's go back to the Garden of Eden, the place of God's original intention for humanity.

RELATIONSHIP AND RESPONSIBILITY: God created the heavens and the earth, the sea, and the animals. He created Adam and Eve to be in relationship with Him and placed them in a garden. He gave them the responsibility to care for His creation and have authority over it. God even spent time presenting each animal to Adam for him to name them.

REBELLION: Adam, Eve and God were in perfect relationship with each other. However, that did not last long. Satan entered the garden and led Adam and Eve astray, causing them — and ultimately all of humanity — to rebel against God. In this act of rebellion, known as original sin, our authority to rule was transferred to satan, and our intimate fellowship with God was severed.

RESCUE: God the Father, being good and wanting a relationship with His children, made a way for us. God revealed our need to be in relationship with Him through the story of the people of Israel. Then He sent His only Son, Jesus, to restore our intimate fellowship. Imagine, the Creator of life entering into creation as a man to live like us and be tempted like us — yet remain sinless; to suffer and die for us on the cross, paying the penalty for our sin; and to rise again to new life, breaking the power of sin and death, and taking back satan's authority over us.

RESTORATION: Intimacy with God has been restored to all who have surrendered to Jesus! While He was victorious over satan at the cross, Jesus is still in the process of bringing about the full restoration of this world. As followers of Jesus, we are invited to partner with God and live in the power of the Holy Spirit to bring about this restoration. Jesus has given us His authority to advance the Kingdom of God here on earth.

RETURN: One day, Jesus will return, and we will live in His Kingdom in all its fullness! The restoration of God's creation will be complete. We are fellow restorers with God, and we carry the King's seal with us wherever we go.

DAILY JOURNAL EXERCISE

What do you think of when you hear the phrase, "Kingdom of God?"

_____

_____

What would it look like for the Kingdom of God to advance in your daily life?

_____

_____

What growth has to happen in you to have His Kingdom come? Should this growth appear in your heart as well as in your actions?

_____

_____

How is God inviting you to be a restorer with Him?

_____

_____

Do you believe God's authority is given to you to do this?

_____

_____

Day 3: God's Prayer List

"This is the confidence we have in approaching God: that if we ask anything according to His will, He hears us." 1 JOHN 5:14 (NIV)

God has a will of His own, and He wants us to participate in it. In the third petition of the Lord's Prayer, Jesus teaches us to pray into the will of God. How do we know what God's will is? We know God's revealed will by reading His written Word, the Bible. It is very important for us to read God's Word on a regular basis to learn and discern God's will. Read this passage of Scripture, revealing the will of God:

"The Spirit of the Sovereign Lord is on me, because the Lord has anointed me to proclaim good news to the poor. He has sent me to bind up the brokenhearted, to proclaim freedom for the captives and release from darkness for the prisoners, to proclaim the year of the Lord's favor and the day of vengeance of our God, to comfort all who mourn, and provide for those who grieve in Zion — to bestow on them a crown of beauty instead of ashes, the oil of joy instead of mourning, and a garment of praise instead of a spirit of despair. They will be called mighty oaks, a planting of the Lord for the display of His splendor. They will rebuild the ancient ruins and restore the places long devastated; they will renew the ruined cities that have been devastated for generations." Isaiah 61:1-4 (NIV)

God's will to restore lives, rebuild the ruins caused by sin and renew His Kingdom here on earth is clearly seen in this passage. What particular qualities can you determine from these verses that God wants to transform in and through us?

_____

_____

We noted in Week One that Jesus prayed into God's will when He fell face down in the Garden of Gethsemane and said, *"My Father! If it is possible, let this cup of suffering be taken away from me. Yet I want your will to be done, not mine." Matthew 26:39.* Through earnest prayer, He submitted to the will of God, being obedient to carry our sins on the cross, so that the Father's desire to reconcile humanity could be accomplished. If we are to partner with God's will, it requires obedience from us as well. Remember that our Father's will for us is always good. Ultimately, it's the best pathway for our lives, although it may be difficult at times.

DAILY JOURNAL EXERCISE

Read Romans 12:1-2 (NASB):

"Therefore I urge you, brethren, by the mercies of God, to present your bodies a living and holy sacrifice, acceptable to God, which is your spiritual service of worship. And do not be conformed to this world, but be transformed by the renewing of your mind, so that you may prove what the will of God is, that which is good and acceptable and perfect."

According to this passage, how are we to worship God?

_____

_____

Is there any dream or desire in your life that you need to submit to God's will?

_____

_____

What qualities from Isaiah 61:1-4 would you like the Holy Spirit to transform in you?

_____

_____

Invite God to begin this work in you so you can more fully serve Him and live for His glory.

_____

_____

Pray for others: Pick a friend or a family member and commit to praying for them regularly. Ask God how He would like to reveal His goodness to that person through you? Name: _____

DAY 4: STAYING CONNECTED

"But Jesus often withdrew to the wilderness for prayer." LUKE 5:16

Heaven is the place where God's will is done perfectly. There is no rebellion in Heaven. There are no restraints or restrictions to worshipping God freely. It is a place of perfect fellowship with God and each other. This is our ultimate destination as believers, and Jesus invites us to pull Heaven to earth now through fervent prayer.

Jesus brought Heaven to earth during His earthly ministry by healing the sick, calming the storms, delivering the oppressed and raising the dead (Luke 8). Yet, as we read the Gospels, we see a striking contrast between the dramatic public encounters of Jesus and His hidden life in prayer (Luke 5:15-16). As crowds pressed in on Jesus, eager to draw from His power, He often withdrew from them to solitary places where He would seek the Father's voice and the Holy Spirit's refreshing. Jesus maintained His connection with God.

If we want to change our world, then we must learn this correlation between the authority of Jesus in ministry and His intimacy with God in prayer. Our lives are demanding, and there are needs all around us. We long to see God move in power, but are we willing to follow Jesus into solitary places of prayer where we can connect with our Father in Heaven and be filled with the Spirit's power?

Jesus had a rhythm of life that prioritized spending time with God in prayer. He got up early to pray. He went off by Himself to pray. Time spent with the Father was the primary vehicle for determining the outcomes and events of His day. In order to learn God's will, both for our own lives and for those around us, we need to draw near to Him regularly. As Jesus said in John 15:5, *"Yes, I am the vine; you are the branches. Those who remain in me, and I in them, will produce much fruit. For apart from me you can do nothing."*

DAILY JOURNAL EXERCISE

Take a brief inventory of your life rhythms — the day, the week and the month. Are you intentionally setting aside time to connect with your heavenly Father in prayer?

_____

_____

Is God speaking to you about how you might create space in your life to be with Him?

_____

_____

Read Matthew 7:9-11 (NASB):

> "Or what man is there among you who, when his son asks for a loaf, will give him a stone? Or if he asks for a fish, he will not give him a snake, will he? If you then, being evil, know how to give good gifts to your children, how much more will your Father who is in Heaven give what is good to those who ask Him!"

Do you believe your Father wants to give gifts to you by His Spirit?

_____

Pray for God's presence and power to fall afresh on your life today. Ask God to pour His gifts in and through you, so that His love can be demonstrated to those around you.

_____

_____

Pray for others: Continue praying for your friend or family member. Has God shown you how He wants to use you to demonstrate His goodness to this person?

DAY 5: LISTENING TO GOD'S VOICE

"All Scripture is inspired by God and is useful to teach us what is true and to make us realize what is wrong in our lives. It corrects us when we are wrong and teaches us to do what is right." 2 TIMOTHY 3:16

Praying into God's will requires listening to His voice. There's an old monastic tradition developed by St. Benedict, a practice of "listening with the ear of our hearts." This practice, called Lectio Divina or "Holy Reading," allows us to be fully present in a heart-centered way, as God's voice speaks to us through the words of Scripture. Listening deeply to the text, we enter into an encounter with God where our hearts are illuminated by a fresh "Word" delivered through Scripture. Just as light shimmers across a field after the clouds are swept away by the sun, so God's Word shimmers within our hearts as we meditate on it.

The four movements of Lectio Divina — read, reflect, respond and rest — reveal the natural opening of our spirits in prayer. As we read God's Word, we then enter into reflection on what He is saying to us and respond to His invitation. Finally, we rest in His presence — content to be still with God, letting His radiance shine over us. In this state of receiving from the Holy Spirit, we are transformed.

"They can be like a sun, words. They can do for the heart what light can for a field."
JOHN OF THE CROSS, LOVE POEMS FROM GOD

"Prayer is not our trying to change God's mind. It is learning what is the mind of God and asking accordingly. (1 John 5:14-15); We must be ready to listen at all times, because He may be ready to speak at any time. (Psalm 16:7-11)"
CHARLES STANLEY

DAILY JOURNAL EXERCISE

Practice Lectio Devina today. Let's read Luke 10:1-9, or pick your own passage:

"The Lord now chose seventy-two other disciples and sent them ahead in pairs to all the towns and places He planned to visit. These were His instructions to them: 'The harvest is great, but the workers are few. So pray to the Lord who is in charge of the harvest; ask Him to send more workers into His fields. Now go, and remember that I am sending you out as lambs among wolves. Don't take any money with you, nor a traveler's bag, nor an extra pair of sandals. And don't stop to greet anyone on the road.

'Whenever you enter someone's home, first say, May God's peace be on this house. If those who live there are peaceful, the blessing will stand; if they are not, the blessing will return to you. Don't move around from home to home. Stay in one place, eating and drinking what they provide. Don't hesitate to accept hospitality, because those who work deserve their pay.

'If you enter a town and it welcomes you, eat whatever is set before you. Heal the sick, and tell them, The Kingdom of God is near you now.'"

READ: The first stage is LECTIO (reading) where we read the Word of God slowly and reflectively so that it sinks into us. Read the passage two or three times, allowing yourself to pause and stop over words or ideas that stand out or "shimmer."

REFLECT: The second stage is MEDITATIO (reflection) where we think about the text and ruminate on it so that we glean from it what God wants to give us. Look at the text from different angles. Ask who, what, when, where and why questions to get beneath the surface.

RESPOND: The third stage is ORATIO (response). Ask the Lord to respond to you in the midst of this passage. What does He want you to hear? What is He trying to tell you? Allow the Word of God to become living and active in your life.

REST: The final stage is CONTEMPLATIO (rest) where we rest in the presence of God. Take time in this stage. Don't rush. Just sit with God in silence. Allow His peace and presence to fill you. Allow the Holy Spirit to transform you.

Week Five

Give Us Today

our

Daily Bread

WEEK FIVE

"GIVE US TODAY OUR DAILY BREAD" MATTHEW 6:11 (NIV)

Petition and Thanksgiving

"Nothing pleases God more than when we ask for what He wants to give. When we spend time with Him and allow His priorities, passion and purpose to motivate us, we will ask for things that are closest to His heart."
BRUCE WILKERSON

▶◀ Watch this week's video at: www.PrayingLikeJesus.com/week-5

KEY LEARNINGS:

1. God _____ for you as His child. Your needs _____ to Him. *(1 Peter 5:7)*

2. We cannot _____ from God if we do not _____ of Him. *(Matthew 7:7-8)*

3. Prayer doesn't need to be overly _____. God doesn't prioritize _____ concerns over _____ ones. *(Matthew 6:11)*

4. Giving thanks increases our _____ in God's _____. *(1 Thessalonians 5:16-18)*

5. We can be confident that God _____ our prayers when we make our _____ known to Him. *(1 John 5:14-15)*

"Any concern too small to be turned into a prayer is too small to be made into a burden."
CORRIE TEN BOOM

NOTES

DAY 1: GOD CARES

"Give all your worries and cares to God, for He cares about you." 1 PETER 5:7

In Matthew 6:11, Jesus invites us to ask God to meet our daily needs. Consider the way a mama bird cares for her young. Amazingly, she prepares for her offspring's arrival well in advance of her due date. The mama bird prepares a nest for her eggs to hatch. Then she continues to sit on the eggs as a watchful mother, guarding and protecting her unborn. Once her young arrive, the mama busily flies back and forth with food to nourish them.

The incredible point of this process is that the mother knows exactly what her offspring will need, and she begins her preparations well ahead of time. This is a powerful illustration of how our heavenly Father cares for us. He knew us before we were even born (Psalm 139:13-16), and even then, we were of great worth in His eyes. At that moment, He knew all we would ever need and began His preparations for us ahead of time. Our Father already knows what we need, but He loves for us to ask, expressing our childlike faith in Him.

There is nothing too small or too big, insignificant or inconvenient for us to ask of our Father, because He already knows and has prepared all that we will need. The mama bird doesn't provide shelter, food and protection based on what her young does or doesn't do. She provides purely because they are her own. The Father cares for us in this same way. We don't need to perform better, give more or love Him more to gain His approval. He cares and provides for His children simply because we are His own.

He just wants us to come to Him, remembering that He is a good Father, who freely and lovingly gives to His children. Paul put it this way, *"And this same God who takes care of me will supply all your needs from His glorious riches, which have been given to us in Christ Jesus." Philippians 4:19*

DAILY JOURNAL EXERCISE

Is it easy or difficult for you to ask God to meet your needs?

_____

_____

What do you think might be getting in the way of approaching your Father in this manner?

_____

_____

Does it change your perspective to come to God knowing He has provided in advance for all you will need?

_____

_____

Do you believe this is true?

_____

_____

If God already knows what we need, why do you think He wants us to ask Him?

_____

_____

Day 2: Daily Dependence

O most merciful Redeemer, Friend and Brother,
May I know Thee more clearly,
Love Thee more dearly,
And follow Thee more nearly,
day by day.

SAINT RICHARD OF CHICHESTER

Words taken from the Broadway musical Godspell remind us of a daily dependence on our God — to see Him, love Him and follow after Him. The Lord's Prayer teaches us to do the same by encouraging us in a daily dependence as we pursue God's Kingdom. The prayer also instructs us to ask for what we need each day, our "daily bread." This causes us to constantly depend on God for His provision.

The Narnia story, "Prince Caspian," by C.S. Lewis, gives us a great illustration of what our daily dependence on God should look like. When a child encounters Aslan, the Christ figure of the story, after not seeing him for a while, she thinks he has grown. In essence, he hasn't grown at all, but the child has. Aslan reminds her that as she grows, she will find him bigger. The same is true about our walk with God. As we continue to grow in Him and depend on Him, we will find He becomes a much bigger presence in our lives.

As we depend daily on our Father to meet our needs — whether for ourselves or for those around us — we can't help but see God getting bigger in our lives and His unlimited resources being revealed from our limited perspectives. Daily He calls us to bring our needs and cares before Him. As we do, our relationship with God grows, and we mature in our ability to trust in His care. Let's continue our journey to see Him more purposefully, love Him more deeply and follow Him more closely, so that our understanding of God expands and our ability to trust in Him deepens each day.

DAILY JOURNAL EXERCISE

What do you need from your Father today? Talk to God about this.

_____

_____

We are accustomed to making a grocery list when we go to the store. Try making a list of your needs for today. Pray your way down the list, placing each item into God's care.

My needs:

_____

_____

_____

_____

_____

As we depend on our Father and grow in our relationship with Him, is it possible for what we think we need to change over time?

_____

_____

Praying for others: God calls us to pray for one another's needs. Choose a friend or family member. Now try something creative. Get a note card and place their name on it. Then list their needs on the card, and use it to pray for them. Keep this prayer card so you can see how God is answering your prayers in their life.

Day 3: Bread From Heaven

"Keep on asking, and you will receive what you ask for. Keep on seeking, and you will find. Keep on knocking, and the door will be opened to you. For everyone who asks, receives. Everyone who seeks, finds. And to everyone who knocks, the door will be opened." MATTHEW 7:7-8

When Jesus used the word "bread" in this petition, He was certainly referring to our physical sustenance. The Hebrew word for bread meant all kinds of nutrition. It's very difficult to deal with our spiritual health when we are hungry, tired, sick or stressed. As human beings, we are made up of body, soul and spirit. The Lord cares about each aspect of our being. To pray "Give us today our daily bread" is to ask God to meet all our needs — physical, emotional and spiritual — trusting He is there each day as our sole source of supply. R. T. Kendall puts it this way:

"Martin Luther said it [daily bread] meant everything necessary for the preservation of this life: food, a healthy body, good weather, house, home, children, good government — even peace." (R.T. Kendall, "The Lord's Prayer," pp. 118-119)

Just as God provided the Israelites with manna and quail to eat each day while they travelled in the desert, and kept the soles of their shoes from wearing out, so He will provide for all our needs as well, if only we will come to Him and ask. As we ask, we trust that our Father knows best, and are willing to learn that what we thought we needed, we did not actually need after all.

Another significant aspect of this prayer is that Jesus calls us to pray "Give us this day our daily bread." This is not just a personal petition, but a call to intercession for one another. Our eyes should be open to the suffering of those around us, recognizing their needs as our assignment to pray. When we sit down to break bread together, we give thanks, acknowledging that every good gift comes down to us from God our Father (James 1:17). As we give thanks, we also pray for those who do not have food to eat, recognizing that many around the world are in deep need. We are part of a family of brothers and sisters all praying to our heavenly Father together, and we stand ready to be the response to prayers by sharing with one another.

DAILY JOURNAL EXERCISE

How have you seen God's provision in your own life? Consider your physical, financial, relational, emotional and spiritual needs. Think of all the ways God has responded to your needs throughout the years, and spend some time giving thanks to Him for His faithfulness to you. Be grateful for all God has done in your life.

Physical needs:

_____

_____

Financial needs:

_____

_____

Relational needs:

_____

_____

Emotional needs:

_____

_____

Spiritual needs:

_____

_____

Give thanks:

_____

_____

DAY 4: PRACTICING GRATITUDE

"God is not remote from us. He is at the point of my pen, my pick, my paint brush, my needle — and my heart and my thoughts."

PIERRE THEILHARD DE CHARDIN

Five hundred years ago, St. Ignatius of Loyola — a theologian who founded the Society of Jesus (Jesuits) — developed a method of prayerful reflection that not only enriched his own spiritual life, but was intended to be shared with others as well. Ignatius so firmly believed in the value of this prayer exercise that he required the Jesuits to practice the Examen twice daily — at noon and at the end of the day.

Examen comes from a Latin word meaning examination, to weigh or judge something. The subject matter of Examen is your life – specifically the day you've just lived. This method blurs the boundaries between prayer and life as we bring our most recent day before the Lord for review, looking for signs of His presence. Brother Lawrence called this, "practicing the presence of God."

Although different variations of the steps of Examen exist, there are generally five steps:

1. **Become aware of God's presence.**

2. **Give thanks for the day.** Be grateful.

3. **Review the day with God.** Tell Him your thoughts, feelings and experiences.

4. **Respond in prayer.** Ask forgiveness and surrender your weaknesses to God.

5. **Invite Jesus into tomorrow.** Talk with Him about your needs and concerns. Ask for His help.

This ancient prayer has great relevance for us today in learning to connect with God more deeply, practice gratitude and listen to God's voice for our lives.

"Always be joyful. Never stop praying. Be thankful in all circumstances, for this is God's will for you who belong to Christ Jesus."
1 THESSALONIANS 5:16-18

DAILY JOURNAL EXERCISE

Let's practice the steps of Examen.

Become aware of God's presence:

- Ask the Holy Spirit to come and be with you. Perhaps read some Scripture to help you focus your mind.
- Don't rush through this.
- Take the necessary time to find calm in God's presence:

   "Be still and know that I am God!" Psalm 46:10

   "The Lord is near all those who call on Him, yes, to all who call on Him in truth." Psalm 145:18

   "The Lord is good to everyone; He showers compassion on all His creation. All of your works will thank you, Lord, and your faithful followers will praise you." Psalm 145:9-10

Give thanks: Review the day in gratitude:

- As you think back over your day, what causes you to be thankful?
- Focus on these experiences/moments and allow yourself to focus on the goodness and generosity of our Father.
- Thank Him.

Review the day with God: Intentionally review your thoughts, feelings and experiences from throughout the day:

- Looking back over the past 24 hours, what were your interactions with others like? How did you feel throughout the day?
- Hit the pause button on life and reflect on who you are and who He is:

   When or where were you most fully cooperating with God's action in your life? When were you resisting? When did you not even care?

   What habits and life patterns do you notice from the past day?

Respond: Talk to God about what you've realized throughout your day:

- You may need to ask forgiveness, ask for direction, share a concern or resolve to make a change. Allow your observations to guide this time:

   Beginning right now, how do you want to do life differently?

Invite Jesus into tomorrow:

- What patterns do you want to keep the same tomorrow?

   Take time to ask the Lord to aid you in this process.

- What needs do you have for tomorrow?

   Release your concerns to Jesus, putting your trust in Him.

- Ask for His help in facing the challenges ahead.

Day 5: God Hears - A Personal Testimony

"And we are confident that He hears us whenever we ask for anything that pleases Him. And since we know He hears us when we make our requests, we also know that He will give us what we ask for." 1 JOHN 5:14-15

I hope to encourage you through a personal testimony of answered prayer in my life. It's just one "stone of remembrance" in the monument of God's faithfulness to me. A few years ago, on a beautiful Thursday morning in June, I was prayer walking with two friends of mine. We do this little ritual every Thursday morning — walking the sidewalks around the local shopping center, sharing life together and praying for one another. On this day, though, I must confess that I was more whining than praying. After 15 years as a professional artist, I had this unfulfilled desire to write an instructional art book, but I honestly had no idea how to make that happen. So my caring friends took my groanings and rearranged the words into a more noble prayer, asking God to direct my steps and open doors for me according to His purposes for my life. I felt affirmed and very blessed to have such understanding friends. But I did not expect what would happen next.

The following day, as I worked quietly in my art studio behind my home, I received an email at around 1 p.m. from a well-known art publishing company. They wanted to know if I'd be interested in writing a 32-page art instructional book for them. No kidding, the very next day! I wrote the book, and it came out in May of the following year — 11 months after our prayer walk together. At the time of this writing, I'm currently writing my third art instruction book.

I share this story with you to encourage you that God hears your prayers, just as He heard mine. He has a better plan for our lives than we would have ever hoped or imagined. So, cast all your cares on the Lord today, for He cares for you!

A.J. PICARD

"And if God cares so wonderfully for wildflowers that are here today and thrown into the fire tomorrow, He will certainly care for you."
MATTHEW 6:30

DAILY JOURNAL EXERCISE

Are there things that you feel called to do with your life and talents?

_____

_____

Do you have any unfulfilled dreams to lay at God's feet today?

_____

_____

Write a prayer to God today talking to Him about this.

_____

_____

_____

_____

_____

_____

AND

FORGIVE
US
OUR DEBTS,

AS WE ALSO HAVE

FORGIVEN
OUR
DEBTORS.

Week Six

WEEK SIX

"AND FORGIVE US OUR DEBTS, AS WE ALSO HAVE FORGIVEN OUR DEBTORS" MATTHEW 6:12 (NIV)

Confession and Forgiveness

"Darkness cannot drive out darkness; only light can do that. Hate cannot drive out hate; only love can do that."
MARTIN LUTHER KING, JR.

▶◀ Watch this week's video at: www.PrayingLikeJesus.com/week-6

KEY LEARNINGS:

1. Everyone has _____ and _____ _____ of God's standard. *(Romans 3:23-24)*

2. Jesus can _____ us of our sin. We are _____ when we _____ our sins to God. *(1 John 1:8-9)*

3. _____ is God's gift to us to restore _____ with Him. *(Romans 8:1)*

4. God _____ we are going to sin. In His love, He extends _____ to us again and again.

5. Satan _____ us, because he wants us to give up. God _____ us, because He wants us to experience the _____ of forgiveness.

6. We _____ because He first _____. *(Luke 23:34)*

7. Extending forgiveness _____ our spiritual health. *(Matthew 6:14-15)*

"If we want to move from a visitation of God to a habitation, then we must assume responsibility to open the doors of repentance and make a way for the Lord to come in and heal us."
DARRELL FIELDS

NOTES

_____

_____

_____

_____

_____

_____

_____

_____

_____

_____

_____

_____

_____

_____

_____

Day 1: The Freedom of Forgiveness

"For everyone has sinned; we all fall short of God's glorious standard. Yet God, with undeserved kindness, declares that we are righteous. He did this through Christ Jesus when He freed us from the penalty for our sins." ROMANS 3:23-24

"He [Jesus] personally carried our sins in His body on the cross so that we can be dead to sin and live for what is right. By His wounds you are healed." 1 PETER 2:24

These piercing words from Scripture describe the cost of our sin, which drove Christ to the cross. With every act of rebellion, another nail is driven into our King. Don't shrink back from the brutal truth of the Gospel. Embracing it will drive you to greater love for your Savior and hatred of your sin, as you turn and run to the foot of the cross where freedom is found.

We've all sinned. Scripture says it, and God knows it. Yet, God does not require full payment or perfection from us. He only desires repentance. We must acknowledge our sin and confess our need for the blood of Jesus to cleanse us. Christ takes that sin upon Himself and declares us righteous before God. By His wounds, we are healed!

The enemy wants to hinder your intimacy with God. He wants to keep you wrapped in cycles of guilt and shame, feeling as if you could never be forgiven for the sin in your life. But, *"The LORD is slow to anger and filled with unfailing love, forgiving every kind of sin and rebellion"* (Numbers 14:18a). It is the kindness of God that leads us to repentance, and we are set free to live as God intended, in the full light of His mercy and grace.

DAILY JOURNAL EXERCISE

Have you ever really considered the cost of your sin?

_____

_____

Looking back over the past month, are you quick to acknowledge your need for Christ to set you free?

_____

_____

Looking back over the past year, are you getting quicker, staying the same or slowing down in your response to sin?

_____

_____

Do you ever try to do God's part by reaching toward perfection or trying to earn your righteousness?

_____

_____

Ask Jesus today to help speed up the response time between your awareness of sin and running to Him to receive the freedom of forgiveness.

_____

_____

_____

Day 2:
Daily Confession

"If we claim we have no sin, we are only fooling ourselves and not living in the truth. But if we confess our sins to Him, He is faithful and just to forgive us our sins and to cleanse us from all wickedness." 1 JOHN 1:8-9

Jesus teaches His disciples about the Holy Spirit in John Chapters 14-16. He keeps calling the Holy Spirit a gift — a gift for us. And then He describes the work of the Holy Spirit, *"He will convict the world of its sin"* (*John 16:8*). "How is this good?" you might ask. The Holy Spirit comes to make the world feel bad over their sins? Absolutely not.

God's desire is always to reconcile and restore, and the Holy Spirit lets people know when separation between them and God has occurred — in order to restore the relationship once again. Paul underlines this truth in Romans 8:1-2 when he says, *"So now there is no condemnation for those who belong to Christ Jesus. And because you belong to Him, the power of the life-giving Spirit has freed you from the power of sin that leads to death."*

When we initially surrender our lives to Jesus, our salvation is secure through faith in Christ. Yet, there is still a need to practice daily confession of the sins we commit, turning away from them so that we can continue to walk in intimacy with God. The gift of the Holy Spirit is that He lets us know when we have dishonored God. He convicts us so that we can turn back to Him and experience the freedom of forgiveness. By contrast, satan always condemns us, intending to separate us from God, so that we feel hopeless and guilty. Confession is God's gift to us, bringing restoration so that we can come boldly into His presence each day.

DAILY JOURNAL EXERCISE

Receiving forgiveness: Practice confession today. Here are some helpful steps to receive God's forgiveness.

+ Ask the Lord what you have done to displease Him. Allow Him to bring these things to your mind. You do not need to go searching for things. Ask the Holy Spirit to convict you.

+ Confess these things to God. Let Him know you acted wrongly, missed the mark, misrepresented Him and acted out of selfishness.

+ Say you're sorry. Ask the Lord to forgive you for these things. Take the time to fully receive His forgiveness.

+ Ask the Holy Spirit to come and fill you up and empower you to live for God. (Remember, God knows we are going to sin, so there is no need to promise Him that you'll be perfect.)

+ Now you are free to pray boldly before the Lord!

_____

_____

_____

_____

_____

Day 3: No Looking Back

"Forget the former things; do not dwell on the past. See, I am doing a new thing! Now it springs up; do you not perceive it? I am making a way in the desert and streams in the wasteland. … I, even I, am He who blots out your transgressions, for my own sake, and remembers your sins no more."
ISAIAH 43:18-19, 25 (NIV)

How many of us look back at our lives before Jesus and see a wasteland of sinful ruin? I certainly do. Yet, the One who created us has made a promise to do an entirely new thing in and through our lives! When we repent of our sins and turn to Jesus, He blots them out of Heaven's record and remembers them no more (Isaiah 43:25). God does not dwell on our past, and we shouldn't either. The Lord relates to us in light of who we are becoming, not who we were. It is to the glory of God that we are made new, for His grace and mercy are put on display like shimmering streams in the barren desert.

2 Corinthians 5:17 says, *"This means that anyone who belongs to Christ has become a new person. The old life is gone; a new life has begun!"* What a cause for great joy! Let's worship the Lord for His willingness to forgive us, and never look back.

DAILY JOURNAL EXERCISE

Even though you have been made new in Jesus, is there anything about your former life that still nags at you and causes you to feel unworthy or unholy? It's important to talk to God about this. Write these aspects of your old life down on a separate piece of paper. Now look at the list and thank God specifically for each item He has forgiven you for. Thank Him that you have been washed clean of these former sins. Crumple up this paper and throw it away in the garbage. You have been made new, and God has completely cleansed you of this old record. Receive the truth that you are forgiven and made new!

_____

_____

_____

_____

_____

_____

Day 4:
The Prayer with a Condition

"If you forgive those who sin against you, your heavenly Father will forgive you. But if you refuse to forgive others, your Father will not forgive your sins."
MATTHEW 6:14-15

Imagine carrying the immense weight of a multimillion-dollar debt that you could never pay off. The bank is coming to take everything you have and place you in debtors' prison. Your financial situation is hopeless, and you have no means of repayment. At the last moment, the president of the bank walks in and announces that you can forget it all. He has cancelled your debt; you will stay out of prison! Now, to celebrate, you go out and drag your neighbor into people's court because he owes you $100 but doesn't have the means to pay you back.

This is the very startling story that Jesus depicts about the Kingdom of God in Matthew 18:21-35. The image of the first man who had a debt well beyond his ability to pay is a picture of our sinful state, and Jesus is the one who comes and cancels the debt. As people who have received forgiveness, Jesus now calls us to extend forgiveness to others. We are citizens of Heaven, representing Jesus to this world, and He is a God who forgives.

Are you ready to pray for the Lord to forgive you to the degree that you have forgiven others?

DAILY JOURNAL EXERCISE

Read through the whole story of Matthew 18:21-35.

Take time to reflect on this parable. What has your pattern been? Are you a person who quickly moves to extend forgiveness, or are you a person who holds strong grudges?

_____

_____

_____

_____

Ask the Lord to begin to soften your heart and quicken the time from initial offense to extending forgiveness.

_____

_____

_____

_____

Day 5: Representing Jesus

"Father, forgive them, for they don't know what they are doing." LUKE 23:34A

It's very difficult to forgive those who have acted unjustly, committed evil or caused harm toward you. It is especially difficult when they don't see the error of their ways and do not ask for forgiveness. But extending forgiveness toward those who have wounded us is freeing and releases the toxic weight of bitterness that builds up inside us. Therefore, we must forgive others to maintain our own spiritual health and relationship with God.

Jesus, our great King, was nailed to a cross — carrying the unfathomable weight of our sins, as well as the horror of being separated from His Father. Yet, in that moment, He uttered these words to those who crucified Him, *"Father, forgive them, for they don't know what they are doing."* He did not wait for anyone to ask for forgiveness; He simply extended it. And Jesus calls us to do the same.

Harboring unforgiveness creates an open door to allow bitterness, anger and even hate to grow in our hearts. How do we extend forgiveness to people who have hurt and wounded us? How do we live in freedom from the toxic effects of bitterness, rage and malice? Forgiveness is a conscious choice in our pursuit of Jesus. We forgive others because Christ has forgiven us.

DAILY JOURNAL EXERCISE

Extending forgiveness: It's time to forgive those who have hurt you. Here are some steps that may help you as you do the difficult work of releasing forgiveness to others:

- Ask the Holy Spirit to come be with you. Ask Him to reveal to you if there is anyone who you need to forgive.

- Allow yourself to acknowledge the amount of hurt or the deep scars the person left. (Allow yourself to feel the gravity of the hurt, anger, rejection or bitterness … Don't rush this.)

- Now, reconnect your heart to the forgiveness Jesus extends to you. In the same manner, pass on what you have experienced.

- Declare forgiveness toward the individual, institution or group. (This may sound like, "God I forgive [person's name] for [insert hurt/wrong doing] in the same way that you have forgiven me when I have done wrong.")

- Now, ask for the Lord to bless them.

 Week Seven

AND
LEAD
US
✤ NOT INTO ✤
TEMPTATION
BUT
DELIVER US
FROM THE EVIL ONE

WEEK SEVEN

"AND LEAD US NOT INTO TEMPTATION, BUT DELIVER US FROM THE EVIL ONE." MATTHEW 6:13 (NIV)

Spiritual Warfare

"The only way to learn a strong faith is to endure great trials. We learn faith by standing firm amid the most severe of tests."
GEORGE MUELLER

▶◀ Watch this week's video at: www.PrayingLikeJesus.com/week-7

KEY LEARNINGS:

1. God _____ us, because He wants us to _____. The enemy _____ us because he wants us to _____. (*James 1:12-15*)

2. God's purpose for _____ is to make us look more like _____. (*Romans 5:2-5*)

3. We are born onto a battlefield with a real _____ named _____. (*1 Peter 5:8*)

4. God and satan are not _____; satan is a _____ enemy. (*Colossians 2:13b-15*)

5. We are to put on all of God's _____ so we can _____ _____ against the enemy's strategies. (*Ephesians 6:11*)

6. We are called to _____ _____ as a family, _____ for one another in prayer. (*Nehemiah 4:13-14*)

"Pain is never permanent."
SAINT TERESA OF AVILA

DAY 1: GOD IS FOR US

"If God is for us, who can ever be against us?" ROMANS 8:31B

God loves us as His beloved children. Believe it or not, He is our biggest advocate. God is always championing our success and victory, but we do have an enemy who wants to see us stumble and fail. Listen to the words of Jesus in Luke 22:31-32:

"Simon, Simon, satan has asked to sift all of you as wheat. But I have prayed for you, Simon, that your faith may not fail. And when you have turned back, strengthen your brothers." (NIV)

Jesus tells Simon (Peter) that satan has asked to have him. But Jesus replies that He has pleaded in prayer for Peter that his faith would not fail. Then He goes on to tell Peter that when he has repented and turned back to Him, he should go to strengthen his brothers. How amazing that Jesus saw beyond Peter's sin to who he would become in Christ! In Luke 22, we see all this come to pass as Peter denied Jesus three times and fell into sin, but he did not fail completely. In John 21, Peter's relationship to Jesus was restored when He turned back to Jesus and was commissioned to take care of His sheep.

Even though Peter was warned that he was going to deny Christ, it didn't keep him from falling, but it did keep him from failing. Peter knew the availability of forgiveness and that Jesus had prayed for him in his area of weakness. The two things learned from this passage are:

- **Jesus will always provide a way out, as long as we turn to Him.**

- **It's important to pray, on behalf of ourselves and others, for God's power to overcome the trials and temptations that will come along.**

DAILY JOURNAL EXERCISE

Take some time to identify and make a list of the areas where you feel vulnerable, weak and tempted. Then, opposite of those things, list what you need from Jesus to overcome them.

Areas of Weakness and Temptation	**Attribute of Jesus That I Need**

Let the list you made of how to overcome become your prayer list. (For example, if I am tempted to lie in defense of myself when I'm accused, then I need to pray for courage to tell the truth. My prayer will be for courage and truth.)

You can also do this for those you pray for.

Day 2: The Fruit of Suffering

It is very important to remember that God does not tempt us (James 1:12-15). He does, however, test us. Faith is proved true through testing. As we said yesterday, God wants us to succeed, but satan wants us to fail.

What's the purpose of all the trials and suffering we must endure in this life? These verses will shed some light on the subject:

- *1 Peter 1:6-7: "So be truly glad. There is wonderful joy ahead, even though you have to endure many trials for a little while. These trials will show that your faith is genuine. It is being tested as fire tests and purifies gold — though your faith is far more precious than mere gold. So when your faith remains strong through many trials, it will bring you much praise and glory and honor on the day when Jesus Christ is revealed to the whole world."*

- *Romans 5:2-5: ". . . And we boast in the hope of the glory of God. Not only so, but we also glory in our sufferings, because we know that suffering produces perseverance; perseverance, character; and character, hope. And hope does not put us to shame, because God's love has been poured out into our hearts through the Holy Spirit, who has been given to us."*

God's purpose for trials and suffering is revealed. He is conforming us more and more into the image of His son Jesus!

"God is the only One who can make the valley of trouble a door of hope."
CATHERINE MARSHALL

DAILY JOURNAL EXERCISE

You may be in the midst of a trial right now. For the moment, consciously lay it aside and think back to a previous trial that you went through in your life. Ask the Holy Spirit to reveal to you how God used that trial to draw you closer to Himself. How was your faith purified and increased? Were you conformed more into the image of Christ? Describe what that looked like. Let this serve as an encouragement of God's faithfulness to you in the midst of suffering.

_____

_____

_____

_____

_____

Now think about your present trial. Ask the Lord to show you what attribute of His character He wants to reveal and then form in you. How does He want to increase your faith and trust during this time? Pray for a fresh filling of the Holy Spirit, asking the Lord to do these things in and through you.

_____

_____

_____

_____

_____

Day 3: A Real Enemy

We were born onto a battlefield with a real enemy named satan (1 Peter 5:8). One of satan's strategies is to keep as many Christians as possible from realizing their full potential in Christ and mobilizing for battle.

Satan knows that, if we fully believed our identity in Christ, and lived a life of freedom and victory in the power of the Holy Spirit as we daily surrender to Him, he would be running scared. Satan is called the deceiver of the whole world in Revelation 12:7-9:

"Then there was war in Heaven. Michael and his angels fought against the dragon and his angels. And the dragon lost the battle, and he and his angels were forced out of Heaven. This great dragon — the ancient serpent called the devil, or satan, the one deceiving the whole world — was thrown down to the earth with all his angels."

The physical world will often manifest what is happening in the spiritual world. Ephesians 6:12 tells us that we do not battle against flesh and blood, but against evil rulers and authorities of the unseen world, against mighty powers in this dark world, and against evil spirits in the heavenly places. Although we should be aware of this, we are not to be intimidated. Satan is a defeated enemy, for Christ won the victory at Calvary when He broke the power of sin and death. This is not an equal matchup: God is Creator — satan is a created being; God is unlimited in power — satan's power is limited; God is all-knowing — satan has limited knowledge; God speaks only truth — satan is a liar; God is the author of life — satan brings death and destruction; God brings light — satan brings darkness; God gives — satan steals. In this matchup, God is victorious on all counts!

"satan's main strategy – to steal our hearts away from You – to lead us astray from our sincere and pure devotion to You."
SCOTTY SMITH

DAILY JOURNAL EXERCISE

People who are trained to identify counterfeit money only study the real thing — the original. By doing this, they can quickly identify the counterfeit. Satan is a counterfeit, so we want to study the real thing — the attributes of our God. Here's an exercise to get you started:

- Look up Galatians 5:22-23 and make a full list of the fruit of the Spirit.
  "But the Holy Spirit produces this kind of fruit in our lives: love, joy, peace, patience, kindness, goodness, faithfulness, gentleness, and self-control. There is no law against these things!"

- Across from each fruit, write the opposite.

- Use this list as a litmus test to reveal who is operating in the situations of your life. Continue to add to this list as you read through Scripture.

Fruit of the Spirit   **Opposite of the Fruit of the Spirit**

_____   _____

_____   _____

_____   _____

_____   _____

_____   _____

_____   _____

_____   _____

DAY 4:
ARMED FOR
THE BATTLE

"Put on all of God's armor so that you will be able to stand firm against all strategies of the devil." EPHESIANS 6:11

Our daily lives are filled with a number of necessities — sleep, nourishment, personal hygiene, getting dressed, exercise and others — that help us function efficiently in this physical world. There are daily necessities for functioning well spiritually, too, equipping us to take our stand against the devil's schemes.

Take time to read Ephesians 6:10-18.

> "A final word: Be strong in the Lord and in his mighty power. Put on all of God's armor so that you will be able to stand firm against all strategies of the devil. For we are not fighting against flesh-and-blood enemies, but against evil rulers and authorities of the unseen world, against mighty powers in this dark world, and against evil spirits in the heavenly places.
>
> Therefore, put on every piece of God's armor so you will be able to resist the enemy in the time of evil. Then after the battle you will still be standing firm. Stand your ground, putting on the belt of truth and the body armor of God's righteousness. For shoes, put on the peace that comes from the Good News so that you will be fully prepared. In addition to all of these, hold up the shield of faith to stop the fiery arrows of the devil. Put on salvation as your helmet, and take the sword of the Spirit, which is the word of God.
>
> Pray in the Spirit at all times and on every occasion. Stay alert and be persistent in your prayers for all believers everywhere."

DAILY JOURNAL EXERCISE

Dress yourself for the day, by putting on each item:

- **Belt of truth:** I put the Lord's truth around my waist to resist any lies that the enemy might try to speak, and choose to believe that which the Lord has said about Himself and about who I am.

- **Breastplate of righteousness:** I am clothed in the righteousness of Christ. Thank you Jesus for the victory of the cross. I stand boldly before the throne because of what you have done for me.

- **Feet fitted with readiness from the Gospel of peace:** I put on the shoes of the Gospel of peace. Where I walk today, Lord, use me to usher in your Kingdom and your ways.

- **Shield of faith:** Today, I pick up my shield of faith. Lord, would you protect me against any flaming arrows that the enemy tries to throw at me. Lord, thank you that you have placed others with me who are like-minded and battling for your advancement in this world.

- **Helmet of salvation:** On my head, I put on the helmet of salvation. Jesus, you are the one who has saved me. You are the one who I want to focus on. You are the one that I want to be headed toward, so let no distraction turn my head to the right or to the left. Let my eyes simply look for you.

- **Sword of the Spirit, which is the Word of God:** I pick up the Sword of the Spirit. Lord, when I am in the heat of battle today, bring the right Scripture to my mind that I may stand against the enemy and his schemes. Lord, make me more sensitive to you today.

- And **PRAY**

Day 5: Standing Together

"So I (Nehemiah) placed armed guards behind the lowest parts of the wall in the exposed areas. I stationed the people to stand guard by families, armed with swords, spears, and bows. Then as I looked over the situation, I called together the nobles and the rest of the people and said to them, 'Don't be afraid of the enemy! Remember the Lord, who is great and glorious, and fight for your brothers, your sons, your daughters, your wives, and your homes!'"
NEHEMIAH 4:13-14

During the rebuilding of the wall in Jerusalem, Nehemiah stationed the Israelites to stand guard by families day and night, armed with swords, spears and bows (Nehemiah 4:13). As one of Israel's all-time greatest leaders, Nehemiah understood the very real risk of danger, and he responded appropriately by arming the builders with weapons and stationing leaders to stand watch over them. Nehemiah had a strategy for the battlefield.

This is a powerful illustration of our role as Christ-followers who are partnering with God to bring restoration to the world around us (Isaiah 61:4). We must not stand alone but together as a community, fighting side by side to advance His Kingdom here on earth. As the family of God, we are called to stand together by interceding for one another in prayer.

DAILY JOURNAL EXERCISE

We have learned how Ephesians Chapter 6 teaches us to be armed for the battle. Paul encourages us not only to arm ourselves, but to equip one another in Christ's armor as well. Who are you standing beside in prayer on a regular basis, covering one another with the Lord's armor?

Friend 1: _____   Friend 2: _____

If your answer is no one, will you ask the Lord to show you who He wants you to partner with?

_____

_____

We were never meant to walk the Christian life alone. Once you have a name, pray for the courage and boldness to invite this person to lock shields with you in prayer.

_____

_____

_____

_____

_____

May you be fully equipped for the battlefield as you stand together in prayer!

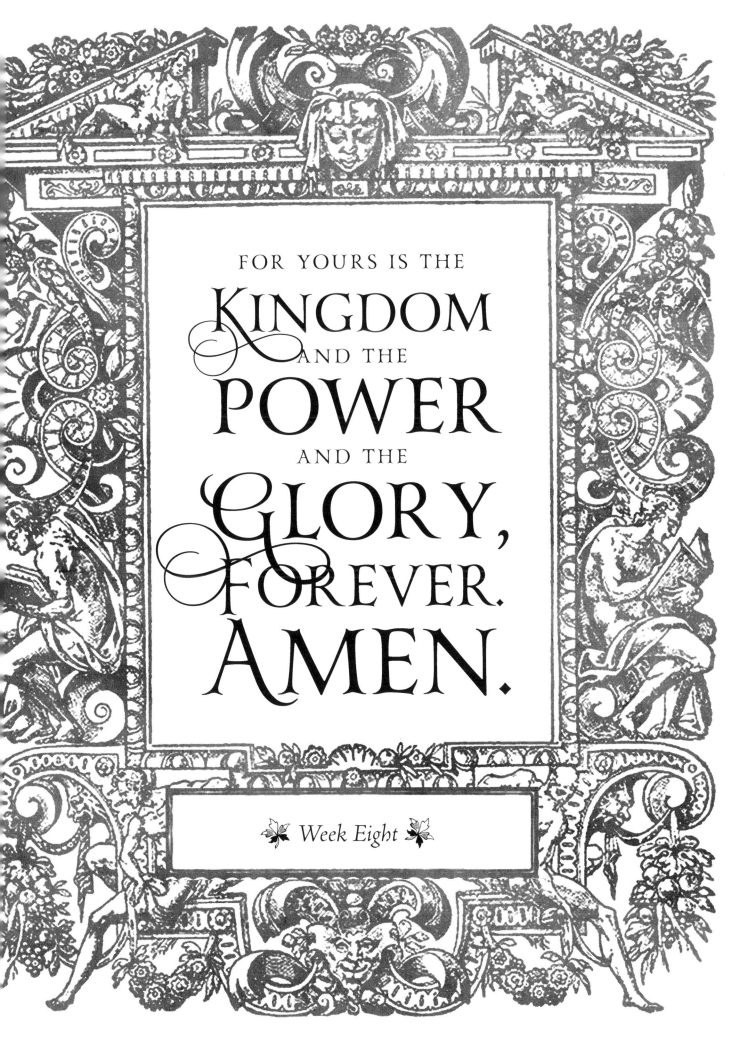

FOR YOURS IS THE

KINGDOM
AND THE
POWER
AND THE
GLORY,
FOREVER.
AMEN.

Week Eight

WEEK EIGHT

"FOR YOURS IS THE KINGDOM AND THE POWER AND THE GLORY, FOREVER. AMEN" MATTHEW 6:13

Proclamation

"Powerful prayer finds its support in the promises of God. When we base our prayers on what God has pledged Himself to do, we stand on unshakable ground."
CHARLES STANLEY

▶◀ Watch this week's video at: www.PrayingLikeJesus.com/week-8

KEY LEARNINGS:

1. We access our _____ in Christ by faith when we _____ the truth of God's Word over our own life and circumstances. *(Ephesians 3:6)*

2. "Yours is the Kingdom" means that God is _____ over all the earth. *(1 Chronicles 29:1)*

3. "Yours is the power" means that God is _____, sustaining all things by His mighty working power. *(Hebrews 1:3)*

4. "Yours is the glory" means that _____ _____ for the glory of God. *(Romans 11:36)*

5. "Forever" means that God is _____. *(Revelation 1:8)*

6. "Amen" declares, "_____, Lord, ____ ___ ___ ___." *(Revelation 7:12)*

"In our home there was always prayer — aloud, proud and unapologetic."
LYNDON B. JOHNSON

NOTES

WEEK 8 : FOR YOURS IS THE KINGDOM AND THE
POWER AND THE GLORY, FOREVER. AMEN.

Day 1:
A Declaration of
Dependence

"So Christ has truly set us free." GALATIANS 5:1

The closing benediction to the Lord's Prayer is a true declaration. Here in America, we commemorate another declaration each Fourth of July when the Declaration of Independence was signed back in 1776. On this national holiday, known as "Independence Day," we honor men like Thomas Jefferson, John Adams and Benjamin Franklin for taking a noble stand and drafting the words that would declare our freedom from the British Empire. Among the lines of this document is one of the best known sentences in the English language — a declaration that has had profound implications on human rights for generations to follow:

"We hold these truths to be self-evident, that all men are created equal, that they are endowed by their Creator with certain unalienable Rights, that among these are Life, Liberty and the pursuit of Happiness."

The American Revolutionary War began in 1775, but the final defeat of Britain did not come until eight years later when the Treaty of Paris was signed on September 3, 1783, giving lasting independence to the United States. This Declaration of Independence was made eight full years before our country was actually set free from British rule. Freedom was gained through the tremendous sacrifice of those with the courage and fortitude to give their lives in pursuit of this cause.

How true this is of our spiritual lives as well. We must make a declaration before freedom is ever won in our hearts and lives. Jesus made the first declaration when He said, "It is finished," breathing His last breath from the cross. The power of sin and death were broken in that pivotal moment, as the perfect Lamb of God was sacrificed for the sins of the world.

Ours is a different kind of declaration. It is a declaration of *dependence* on Jesus, as we surrender our lives to Him. We are Christ's regenerate band of freedom fighters here in New England, believing that our mission is to declare freedom in Christ over our cities and towns, and our friends and families — to take a bold stand on behalf of prisoners of darkness that they may be set free. Victory over darkness has already been won at the cross, and we battle from victory not for it.

Are you discouraged by having seen great pain and suffering around you? Are you tired from the battlefield of life? Never forget that a declaration of freedom has already been made over us, and the battle is already won in Jesus. Ours is to persevere in establishing the Kingdom of Heaven here on earth, anticipating the return of our great King. "For Yours is the Kingdom and the Power and the Glory" is our Declaration of Dependence on King Jesus, our Lord.

DAILY JOURNAL EXERCISE

Praying out loud:

God hears our prayers, no matter whether we pray silently in our thoughts, write them down, speak them out loud or even sing them. Although all these forms of prayer are great, it's important to develop a comfort level praying out loud. Let's practice this today by taking a walk outside or going to a place where you won't disturb anyone with your voice and praying out loud. Proclaim God's goodness to Him, speak out words of truth from Scripture, and thank God for His promises. Read a Psalm out loud to God if you're not sure what to say. When we proclaim God's goodness out loud, we change the atmosphere around us and within us. Here's an example of what a prayer of proclamation can look like:

"Lord, I declare that you are a good Father, and that your plans for me are good, as one of your beloved children. I declare that all things are working together for good in my life because I love you and I am called according to your purposes in Christ Jesus. I will fully put my trust in your good purposes today. I declare that no weapon formed against me will prosper in any way, for I am hidden under your watchful care, Lord. Thank you for your faithfulness to me. Your ways are higher than my ways, your thoughts are higher than my thoughts, and your plans are better than my plans could ever be. I declare that you are the living God who loves me and daily makes a way for me."

A proclamation prayer found in Scripture:

"Now all glory to God, who is able to keep you from falling away and will bring you with great joy into His glorious presence without a single fault. All glory to Him who alone is God, our Savior through Jesus Christ our Lord. All glory, majesty, power, and authority are His before all time, and in the present, and beyond all time! Amen." Jude 1:24-25

Day 2:
Declaring the Promise

"What joy for those whose strength comes from the Lord, who have set their minds on a pilgrimage to Jerusalem. When they walk through the Valley of Weeping, it will become a place of refreshing springs. The autumn rains will clothe it with blessings. They will continue to grow stronger, and each of them will appear before God in Jerusalem." PSALM 84:5-7

In difficult seasons, we rise above the harsh reality of our struggles by setting our sights on a greater reality — the promise of our eternal inheritance in Christ. Our local community endured the Sandy Hook Elementary School shooting in December, 2012. When a prominent pastor visited our grieving church to minister us, he said, "The valley is not your permanent home." Difficult times invite us to declare the truth of Scripture over our current circumstances, looking to Jesus as our hope-bringing force in the midst of the struggle.

This passage tucked away in Psalm 84 can become a *kairos* word — a fresh word — to proclaim over your own life and circumstances. Like the psalmist, we are a people on a pilgrimage to seek God's face and gain His direction for our lives. God invites us to claim the promise that our own "Valley of Weeping" will be transformed into a place of refreshing springs. If you find yourself in the valley, then I challenge you to declare these words over your own life, so that the autumn rains of His presence may come and clothe you with blessings, for God is with you, and He is mighty to save.

DAILY JOURNAL EXERCISE

What promises are you holding onto that have not yet been fulfilled in your life? It could be a promise of salvation for a loved one, a promise of healing for an illness, a promise of transformation in a family member, or a breakthrough in your life circumstances. For each promise, it is powerful to find a Scripture that speaks a truth into that promise, giving you fresh faith to persevere in prayer.

Write down the promise God has revealed to you in the space on the left. Then find Scriptures to empower your prayers, and place the verses on the right.

God's Promise to You	Scripture Related to the Promise

"I will never leave you or forsake you"
DEUTERONOMY 31:8

Day 3: Returning to Worship

Among Christian traditions, a doxology is typically an expression of praise sung to the Father, Son and Holy Spirit.

The doxology at the end of The Lord's Prayer appears in about half the of the 6,000 full or partial New Testament manuscripts existing from early times. Although this is a cause for controversy, scholars have a deep appreciation for the placement of the doxology at the end of the Lord's Prayer, as it returns us to worship, directing our focus back to God. Let's take a closer look at the makeup of these final words:

- YOURS IS THE KINGDOM: Beginning with the possessive pronoun "Yours" declares that God is sovereign over all the earth. His Kingdom is not a democracy. Whether we "vote" for Him or not, Jesus is still the King. This affirms our surrender once more, giving Jesus and His Kingdom rule over our lives.

- YOURS IS THE POWER: The Greek word used for power here is *dunamis* — the same word from which we get dynamite. God possesses all power in Heaven and on earth — creative power, saving power and transforming power. This explosive power comes as we invite the work of the Holy Spirit to move in

and through us. Here, we affirm that God is omnipotent, sustaining all things by His mighty working power. We worship and bow low before the all-powerful One who holds our lives in His hands.

- YOURS IS THE GLORY: The great musical composer, Johann Sebastian Bach, used to write the initials "S.D.G." at the bottom of all his musical compositions to remind himself — and all those after him who would play his works — that God alone was to receive the glory. These initials stood for the Latin phrase, *"Soli Deo Gloria,"* which means "Glory to God alone."

Everything exists for the glory of God to reveal His majesty, holiness, goodness and grace. In this affirmation, we dwell on the character of God once again. As the moon reflects the light of the sun, so we ought to reflect the glory of God forever. Paul used similar language in Romans 11:36 when he declared these words, *"For everything comes from Him and exists by His power and is intended for His glory. All glory to Him forever!"*

DAILY JOURNAL EXERCISE

Here's another well-known Protestant doxology originating from the Lutheran Church:

Praise God, from whom all blessings flow;
Praise Him, all creatures here below;
Praise Him above, ye heavenly host;
Praise Father, Son and Holy Ghost. Amen.

Why not try writing your own doxology as a way of praising God? Whose kingdom are you building? Whose career, reputation and wealth are you working for? Whose power are you relying on today? Finally, whose glory are you living for in your relationships, your words and the work of your hands? Flesh this out in your own prayer of praise to God.

_____

_____

_____

_____

_____

_____

"Worship is a lifestyle. It is not part of your life; it is your life. How is this possible? By doing everything as if you were doing it for Jesus and by carrying on a continual conversation with Him while you do it ... The heart of worship is surrender ... We give ourselves to Him, not out of fear or duty, but in love, because He first loved us." (John 4:9-10, 19)
RICK WARREN

Day 4: Agreeing with God

The final two words of the doxology at the close of the Lord's Prayer conclude our eight-week journey of apprenticing with Jesus.

Let's delve into their significance for us:

+ FOREVER: Forever declares that God's sovereignty, omnipotence and glory are not temporary but eternal, reaching from everlasting to everlasting. He is the Alpha and the Omega, the first and the last.

+ AMEN: We are so accustomed to ending our prayers with amen, that we may think of it as nothing more than a way of signing off with God, or a kind of verbal punctuation. In fact, amen is an Old Testament word. It is derived from Aramaic, and means "truly" or "so be it." Having prayed according to Jesus' instructions, now we declare, "yes, Lord, let it be so." Amen is more than mere punctuation to the Lord's Prayer; it is a declaration of our agreement with God that His will, His ways, His thoughts and His plans are right and true.

Do you recall King David's prayer from Week Three (Day Three)? He prayed a prayer in his day that resonates with uncanny similarity to the closing benediction of the Lord's Prayer.

David said, "*Yours, O Lord, is the greatness, the power, the glory, the victory, and the majesty. Everything in the heavens and on earth is yours, O Lord, and this is your Kingdom. We adore you as the one who is over all things.*" *1 Chronicles 29:11*

We can agree that this kind of prayer pleases the Lord. The disciples asked Jesus to teach them to pray, desiring to unlock the secrets of His amazing prayer life that resulted in such an extraordinary ministry on earth. So He did, giving them a pattern to pray in the Lord's Prayer.

DAILY JOURNAL EXERCISE

Think back over the past eight weeks of apprenticing with Jesus in prayer. How has your relationship with God changed?

_____

_____

_____

Which aspects of the Lord's Prayer had the most significant impact on you?

_____

_____

_____

Which parts did you struggle with?

_____

_____

_____

Where do you think there is more room for growth with God?

_____

_____

_____

DAY 5: AN UNWAVERING LIFESTYLE

"But when Daniel learned that the law had been signed, he went home and knelt down as usual in his upstairs room, with its windows open toward Jerusalem. He prayed three times a day, just as he had always done, giving thanks to his God." DANIEL 6:10

Allow me to set the scene for you. It's just another day at the office, and you are faithfully going about your business. Then you step away from your desk to get a coffee when suddenly crisis strikes. You discover that co-workers are conspiring against you to get you fired, bringing accusations before your boss to implicate you for violating company policy. Think quick! What do you do ... get even, shout louder, run?

This is the story of Daniel who was thrown into the lion's den. Read all of Daniel Chapter 6 for the whole exciting story. We remember the scene where God delivers Daniel from the persecution of his peers and the jaws of hungry lions. But let's focus on a different aspect of the story, for the key to Daniel's victory is tied to his unwavering lifestyle of prayer.

Daniel's rhythm of meeting with God had been established early in life and protected throughout his professional service to the King. Jealousy among colleagues caused them to try to frame Daniel as a religious violator for continuing these spiritual disciplines to the God of Israel. What strikes me as so poignant is the nature of Daniel's heroism. When confronted with crisis, he does nothing new or exciting.

In fact, he does ... the usual. Daniel turned to prayer, just as he had always done.

The treasure for you and I to glean lies in Daniel's spiritual disciplines. Far before crisis struck and before jealous adversaries sought to remove him from office, Daniel established himself in the Lord with a consistent rhythm of prayer. Daniel knew God. In fact, he met with Him three times a day. And when Daniel was thrown into a lion's den, do you know who showed up to hang out with him? God. I suspect He didn't want to miss their usual appointment, even if it was relocated to a lion's den. Daniel did not turn to God in crisis alone. He turned to God every day with whatever was on his heart, big or small, remembering to always give thanks.

As we close our journey together, it's inspiring to look at a hero from Scripture to inspire us to go deeper in our relationship with God. May you be like Daniel and develop a rich intimacy with the Lord that is rooted in regular times of meeting with Him. And when those trials come again, it'll be wonderful to have the God of Heaven on your side!

Closing Thoughts

What an incredible journey this has been together. We've unpacked the model prayer line by line over the past eight weeks, as we've sought to apprentice with Jesus in learning to pray. I truly believe that your relationship with God has been greatly enriched as a result.

The Lord's Prayer is designed to be a circular prayer, meaning that you can return to the beginning and pray it all over again, each time encountering God in a fresh way through its familiar pattern. Now, as you move forward from this prayer course, may you be blessed with a rich, authentic and vibrant relationship with your heavenly Father, King Jesus and the Holy Spirit.

AJ PICARD, PASTOR OF PRAYER

WALNUT HILL COMMUNITY CHURCH

BETHEL, CT

"Where there is much prayer, there will be much of the Spirit; where there is much of the Spirit, there will be ever-increasing power."
ANDREW MURRAY

ANSWER KEY

WEEK ONE

APPRENTICING WITH JESUS   10

1. talking, listening
2. view, relate
3. real
4. personal
5. relationship
6. pattern, communion

WEEK TWO

INTIMACY WITH GOD   24

1. image
2. relationship
3. family
4. good
5. chosen, belong

WEEK THREE

ADORATION AND PRAISE   38

1. identity, reputation
2. inspire, praise
3. love, adoration
4. behold, like
5. presence

WEEK FOUR

INTERCESSION AND LISTENING
TO GOD'S VOICE   52

1. domain, surrender
2. intimacy, authority
3. restore, authority
4. will, will
5. spending time, alone, prayer
6. His Word

WEEK FIVE

PETITION AND THANKSGIVING   66

1. cares, matter
2. receive, ask
3. spiritual, spiritual, physical
4. faith, provision
5. hears, requests

WEEK SIX

CONFESSION AND FORGIVENESS   80

1. sinned, fallen short
2. cleanse, forgiven, confess
3. Confession, intimacy
4. knows, mercy
5. condemns, convicts, freedom
6. forgive, forgave
7. restores

WEEK SEVEN

SPIRITUAL WARFARE   94

1. tests, succeed, tempts, fail
2. trials, Jesus
3. enemy, satan
4. equal, defeated
5. armor, stand firm
6. stand together, interceding

WEEK EIGHT

PROCLAMATION   108

1. inheritance, proclaim
2. sovereign
3. omnipotent
4. everything exists
5. eternal
6. Yes, let it be so

Book Recommendations

- "Red Moon Rising: How 24-7 Prayer Is Awakening a Generation," by Pete Greig and Dave Roberts
- "God on Mute," by Pete Greig
- "The Lord's Prayer," by R. T. Kendall
- "Praying the Lord's Prayer," by J.I. Packer
- "The Prayer of the Lord," by R.C. Sproul
- "You Shall Know the Truth," by Ben Woodward
- "Prayer: Finding the Heart's True Home," by Richard Foster
- "Prayer: Does It Make Any Difference?" by Philip Yancey
- "Abba's Child: The Cry of the Heart for Intimate Belonging," by Brennan Manning
- "Restored," by Neil Anderson
- "Total Forgiveness," by R. T. Kendall
- "Alive in the Spirit," by Clive Calver
- "Dying to Live," by Clive Calver
- "Dreaming With God: Co-laboring With God for Cultural Transformation," by Bill Johnson
- "A Simple Life-Changing Prayer: Discovering the Power of S. Ignatius Loyola's Examen," by Jim Manney
- "Lectio Divina — The Sacred Art: Transforming Words & Images into Heart-Centered Prayer," by Christine Valters Paintner

Made in the USA
Monee, IL
16 April 2023

31951799R00074